A DOME OF MANY COLORS

A DOME OF MANY COLORS

STUDIES IN RELIGIOUS PLURALISM, IDENTITY, AND UNITY

Edited by
Arvind Sharma and
Kathleen M. Dugan

TRINITY PRESS INTERNATIONAL
Harrisburg, Pennsylvania

Cover design: Jim Gerhard
Cover art: Hélice by Robert DeLaunay/Christie's Images/SuperStock

Trinity Press International, P.O. Box 1321, Harrisburg, PA 17105
Trinity Press International is a division of the Morehouse Group.

Library of Congress Cataloging-in-Publication Data
A dome of many colors : studies in religious pluralism, identity, and
    unity / edited by Arvind Sharma and Kathleen M. Dugan.
        p.   cm.
    Includes bibliographical references and index.
    ISBN 1-56338-267-9 (pbk. : alk. paper)
    1. Religious pluralism – Congresses.   I. Sharma, Arvind.
II. Dugan, Kathleen Margaret.
BL60.D65   1999
291.1′72 – dc21   99-13093

Printed in the United States of America

99   00   01   02   03   04   10   9   8   7   6   5   4   3   2   1

Contents

Introduction   1

1. Living in Two Worlds: A Personal Appraisal   7
   Julia Ching

2. Religious Identity and Pluralism   23
   Raimon Panikkar

3. "Our Religions" in a Religiously Plural World   48
   Harvey Cox, Arvind Sharma,
   Seyyed Hossein Nasr, and Masao Abe

4. Civilizing the Choctaws: Cultural Expectations   71
   and Realities
   Clara Sue Kidwell

5. Religious Conflict   88
   Samuel Ruiz Garcia

6. Religion and Globality: Can Interreligious Dialogue   104
   Be Globally Responsible?
   Paul F. Knitter

7. Two Types of Unity and Religious Pluralism   137
   Masao Abe and Donald W. Mitchell

8. Religion, Globality, and Universality   152
   Seyyed Hossein Nasr

9. Summation: Call to Action   179
   Robert J. Schreiter

Contributors   195

Index   197

Introduction

What is religious pluralism? Religious pluralism is a misnomer for religious diversity. The word *diversity* does not lend itself easily to the formation of an abstract noun with an *ism* attached to it. The academic world loves *isms* (altruism, communism, etc.) and feels far more comfortable in dealing with them than with *ities* (as in unity, variety, diversity). Hence it prefers the word *plurality* to *diversity* because it can get an *ism* out of it: pluralism. It would be churlish to point out that, strictly speaking, plurality is an inexact synonym for diversity. Several clones, for instance, would constitute a plurality without constituting a diversity. But as it is too fine a point we shall not make it here but would prefer to advert to a similar terminological tangle represented by the expression "The History of Religions." The phrase is really an effort to translate the German *Religionswissenschaft* into English. The translation of this word as the "science of religion" was felt to be too limited in its connotation, failing to convey the intellectual amplitude of the German term. Thus the study of religion is no stranger to the use of expressions which seem to denote one thing but connote something else. Just as "History of Religions" has to be decoded to mean the counterpart of the German *Religionswissenschaft* in the English-speaking world, religious pluralism has to be decoded to mean religious diversity within the English language itself, on account of the grammatical exigencies of forming abstract nouns. It is apparent from the widespread use of the word *pluralism* that, however circuitous the semantic distillation of a sense of diversity from it, the word has come to stay. Nothing can resist the force of a word whose time has come, any more than the idea it embodies can be resisted. Perhaps the same can be said for expressions, and the ideas embodied therein, such as the 1893 World Parliament of Reli-

1

gions or the 1993 Parliament of World's Religions, the latter held in Chicago in commemoration of the former.

In 1993, Robert J. Schreiter of the Catholic Theological Union and Jeffrey Carlson of DePaul University foresightedly organized a conference on religious pluralism, in tandem with the Parliament of the World's Religions. This book garners some of the fruits of this conference.

The papers included here were presented at the Parliament of the World's Religions on the theme of religious pluralism and represent the many variations of that theme — from a melody (as in Julia Ching's autobiographical narrative) to a symphony (as in Robert Schreiter's summation: "Call to Action"). These constitute the overture and the finale.

While Julia Ching deftly weaves and unweaves, like Penelope, the emerging patterns of her religious identity on the warp and woof of Christianity and her Chinese heritage, Raimon Panikkar traces the golden thread of his religious identity, as it embroiders both his commitment to Christianity and his appreciation of Hinduism with such skill, it seems to us, that if that golden thread were removed from the variegated tapestry of his religious life, more than just that thread would be undone. Living in a religiously plural world, Julia Ching grapples with the question of personal identity in terms of religions, and Raimon Panikkar grapples with the question of religious identity in terms of persons living in a religiously plural world. That their personal testaments should amount to public testimonies speaks volumes about the religiously plural worlds we live in, worlds in which intimate reflection and public disclosure go hand in hand.

The next four pieces constitute personal statements in a somewhat different key. They represent the self-reflection of four contributors to the book *Our Religions*, which was published by HarperSanFrancisco (a division of HarperCollins) as its contribution to the centennial celebration of the 1893 World Parliament of Religions. This book was unique inasmuch it introduced readers to seven religions through scholars who belonged to the very traditions they were writing about: Hinduism (Arvind Sharma), Buddhism (Masao Abe), Confucianism (Tu Wei-ming), Taoism (Liu Xiaogan), Judaism (Jacob Neusner), Christianity (Harvey

Cox), and Islam (Seyyed Hossein Nasr). Four of the contributors — Harvey Cox, Arvind Sharma, Seyyed Hossein Nasr, and Masao Abe — were on hand to reflect on how the text of what they wrote about their religion was affected by the *Sitz im Leben:* the presence of a religiously plural world.

With the next set of chapters the book again moves into a new key and tackles the question of how a tradition as a whole, rather than an individual, faces or has faced the issue of religious pluralism. History replaces biography. Clara Sue Kidwell takes us through the pain of seeing a tradition fall by the wayside as a dominant religio-secular tradition proves insensitive to and perhaps intolerant of religious diversity. Samuel Ruiz takes us on an equally painful journey, across a continent and a few centuries further afield, to the encounter of Christianity with religious diversity in South America. Faith is restored by Paul F. Knitter as we see a glimmer of hope that such wrongs may not be perpetrated in the future (and past wrongs may be forgiven or even atoned for) if interreligious dialogue can find a firm anchor in a religiously plural world.

The very fact of the plurality of religions itself throws the issue of a unity underlying the various families of religions (and of the unity among the families) as well as that of a transcendent unity underlying them all, in bold relief. Two prominent non-Christian scholars address these issues in this volume. Masao Abe examines the question of unity underlying a family of religions and that underlying the families themselves, which attracts a response from Donald W. Mitchell. The even broader issue of the transcendent unity of religions — what the concept means and how it relates to modernity — is explored by Seyyed Hossein Nasr, which attracts a special response from Robert Schreiter in his summation, along with other reflections.

His reflections prompt these further reflections on the nature of our calling as students of religious pluralism. Academics are not prophets, but they do like to peer into the future — if not for prophecies, then for patterns. There are emergent patterns, although it is difficult to foresee which will prevail and whether it will prevail by itself or in combination with others. What is striking is that these patterns are of a piece with the range of

patterns encountered in other pluralistic situations, such as those
of multiculturalism or multilingualism.

One may begin by bracketing out the limiting cases, which in
their own opposite ways eliminate the issue of religious pluralism
itself. These are the poles of fundamentalism, for which all pluralism represents nothing but darkness, and universalism, in which
all pluralism is suffused with light, so much so that "even the
light which leads astray is light from heaven." One darkens pluralism beyond recognition, the other beams it out of sight. There
are, however, some options open for those of us who have not
been abducted either by the devil or by divine aliens.

There is, first of all, the melting-pot pattern, made famous
by the American espousal of it. Some have less respectfully referred to it as a cauldron, but the point essentially is that in this
model the distinctions are muted, if not erased, in the interest
of a common identity. The various religions are, however, not
likely to dissolve easily even though globalization and modernity
are powerful solvents. Knitter seems to suggest something along
these lines.

Then there is the salad-bowl pattern. Each religion finds its
place in the setting, and one can relish whatever one likes. Such
eclecticism is much in evidence, different dishes combining to
produce diverse patterns on the plate but not on the table. Julia
Ching and Raimon Panikkar seem to suggest such a feast.

Some, however, have gone back into the kitchen and suggested
a stir-fry model.[1] According to this model, each item retains its
identity but is influenced by being in proximity to the other.
Culinary association affects the taste of each ingredient, without
destroying its identity or compromising its integrity. The contributors to *Our Religions* would seem to favor such a view, as would
Kidwell and Ruiz.

Then there is the mosaic model, if we can lift our eyes from
the dining table to the opulent dining hall in which we are being
feted. All the religions are like beautiful precious tiles on their
own, but they also constitute a pattern along with others. The

---

1. See S. Cromwell Crawford, *Dilemmas of Life and Death: Hindu Ethics in a
North American Context* (Albany: State University of New York Press, 1995), 4.

longevity of the major religions of the world encourages one to think in terms of this metaphor. Seyyed Hossein Nasr may not be entirely out of sympathy with such a perspective.

But perhaps we should also take a look at the glass dome of the dining hall. If it is an inescapable fact of life, illustrated by religious pluralism, that life is enriched by the various hues it offers, is it also not due to an inescapable human condition that

> Life, like a dome of many-colored glass
> Stains the white radiance of eternity?

ARVIND SHARMA
KATHLEEN M. DUGAN

Chapter 1

Living in Two Worlds: A Personal Appraisal

Julia Ching

Finding Identity

The word *identity* refers to sameness, and *sameness*, in turn, refers to some kind of unity. We are speaking here of oneness in the midst of diversity, of permanence in the midst of change. In the human context, we are speaking of personal identity, of that which makes a person what he or she is, both psychologically and sociologically.

We are all born as persons, but our identity as persons, our personality, grows with time and experience and, perhaps also, with some wisdom. A very young child usually refers to himself or herself as others do: for example, as *baby*. With a bit of aging, he or she starts to assert himself or herself by assuming the use of the word *I*. But even for those who have entered adulthood, it is not always easy to be sure of one's identity. At the extreme, one may confuse reality and illusion. Just to cite the Taoist Chuang Tzu's story:

Once Chuang Chou dreamt he was a butterfly, a butterfly flitting and fluttering around, happy with himself and doing as he pleased. He didn't know he was Chuang Chou. Suddenly he woke up and there he was, solid and unmistakable Chuang Chou. But he didn't know if he was Chuang Chou who had dreamt he was a butterfly, or a butterfly dreaming he was Chuang Chou. Between Chuang Chou and a butterfly there must be some distinction!¹

The question "Who am I?" is therefore linked to the other questions: "Am I real?" and "What is real?" Are we the persons we think we are, or are we not playing out roles assigned to us by society? Has not Shakespeare also said: "All the world's a stage, And all the men and women merely players"?²

Self-interrogation is a path to self-knowledge, and self-knowledge has been called the highest aim of philosophy and, one might add, of wisdom. Of course, no man, and no woman, is an island. The problem of identity would not otherwise arise. Basically, it is the problem of the self finding itself. And this does not arise except in community, as the self struggles to understand itself in relation to other selves — in short, to others. We cannot even tell ourselves who we are, without the help of others. To quote the Catholic philosopher Gabriel Marcel:

> When I ask myself, "Who am I, I, who interrogate myself about my own being?" I have ... a more fundamental question ...; it is this, "Am I qualified to answer this question? ... " But such a fear implies an assumption ... that if a legitimate answer can be finally given to the question ..., it cannot be given ... but ... by somebody else.³

Marcel speaks about the fear we face in knowing that we cannot even answer our own question about who we are. To assert one's identity involves first the acceptance of one's self, but with it, also the acceptance, at least in great part, of what others have to say about one's self. This in turn implies the acceptance of others as persons who define ourselves even as selves. It also implies an established community, a network of relationships between the self and others, and, even more basically, an attitude on the part of oneself which is open to others as selves. After all,

---

1. English translation in Burton Watson, *The Complete Works of Chuang Tzu* (New York: Columbia University Press, 1968), 49.
2. *As You Like It*, act II, scene 7, line 139.
3. Gabriel Marcel, *The Mystery of Being* (Chicago: Henry Regnery, 1960), Gateway edition, vol. 1, *Reflection and Mystery*, 182.

> To accept the other is not merely to tolerate him through indifference.... For the other is the experience, through a person, of something alien.... But the sense of the other ...only begins with respect for the other, and what can we respect in the other if one does not first respect it in oneself?... The sense of the other is inseparable from a sense of inwardness. The other is my fellow, "another self."[4]

It is interesting here to pause over the fact that the Hebrews have believed in a God who says, "I am Who am." This God is saying that he tells us his identity, that he does not depend on others, his nonexistent peers, to tell him who he is.

Yahweh, "I am Who am," is of course God's revelation of his own identity, and his identity is also his name. It has been interpreted by specialists to mean especially "I make to be whatever comes to be" — when the verb is understood causatively. So Yahweh is the creator, the Lord of all.

It is interesting that for so many religious believers, Christians, Jews, and Muslims, belief in this God as the one God and Creator is what defines their own existence and identities. The believers are creatures of God, his children, protected by him. And, just as the "name" is so important in many societies, especially in the Near East, we may say that those who believe in God as creator and as Father may claim the protection of his name. God has named himself. Those who believe in him somehow share his name and take on identities that depend upon his own identity.

In the presence of this pronouncement, we may infer two points: namely, that the claim of Yahweh as creator and Lord is implicitly a universal one, since everything outside of Yahweh is his creature, and yet also, that this nevertheless has a particular effect on some people as distinct from other people, since those who acknowledge his identity and lordship may also claim a special relationship to him, in opposition to those who do not. There is thus an inherent ambiguity regarding how one should identify oneself vis-à-vis Yahweh.

---

4. Emmanuel Mounier, *The Character of Man*, trans. R. H. Fuller (New York: Harper, 1956), 218.

Depending on circumstances, most of us might have been "born" into a religious identity; others might have "adopted" it; while still others might remain quite indifferent to any identity that is religious. But the inherent problem of the Creator God is reflected in the historic struggle to identify one people or nation with him, thus depriving the others of what is theologically their divine patrimony as well—the protection of the same God.

Here, it is interesting to me that adolescence and young adulthood is often the time for a parting of ways: for some people to become religious and others to turn their backs on religion. Adolescence, after all, is the time for groping for, and finding, identity. In adolescence, the self-assertion that began in childhood continues to develop, together with growing self-doubt, and therefore, the *identity crisis:*

> [It] occurs in that period of the life cycle when every youth must forge for himself some central perspective and direction, some working unity, out of the effective remnants of his childhood and the hopes of his anticipated adulthood.[5]

And then there are the groups to which we all belong: families, countries, language, racial and ethnic groups, and also churches and religions. They give us identity, telling us what we are, as well as what we are not. They help us cope with ourselves and with others, with life, with society, with nature. They also complicate our lives, sometimes immensely. In these days of ethnic and religious conflicts and hatreds, many of us — some much more than others — find ourselves caught in a trap not of our own building, which could even be a death trap, be that in Northern Ireland, in Central Asia, in the Middle East, or in the Balkans.

The psychoanalyst Carl Jung turned away from the institutional religion of his parents, even if he remained, in his own way, religious. He said of his own school years:

> Somewhere deep in the background I always knew that I was two persons. One was the son of my parents, who went to school and was less intelligent..., hard-working..., and

---

5. Erik H. Erikson, *Young Man Luther: A Study in Psychoanalysis and History* (New York: W. W. Norton, 1962), 14.

clean than many other boys. The other was grown up — old, in fact — skeptical, mistrustful, remote from the world of men, but close to nature, the earth, the sun, the moon, the weather, all living creatures, and above all close to the night, to dreams, and to whatever "God" worked directly in him.[6]

I recall becoming conscious of the world around me during the Japanese invasion of China. I grew up with a consciousness of my national identity. My teenage fantasies were those of becoming another Hua Mulan, a semilegendary figure who dressed as a boy and joined the army in place of her aging father.[7] She is the Chinese equivalent of France's Joan of Arc. In real life, what I had to cope with was growing up in a complex Chinese family that was struggling to survive in difficult circumstances. The first big decision I made for myself was a religious one. I became a Christian, receiving baptism at a Catholic school while in my mid-teens. At the time, I was not turning my back on whatever values I had learned at home. But I was searching for certitude and commitment, and felt then that faith was the answer.

The biggest mental obstacle to my conversion was my puzzle over the eternal destiny of my own ancestors. Coming from a tradition so identified with the ancestral past, I wondered whether all my ancestors would have perished in hell or were perhaps permitted to remain in purgatory, that place of penitence otherwise reserved for Catholic Christians. Conversion was in a sense a rupture, tearing me apart from my acknowledged identity associated with a venerable ancestral tradition.

At that time, my decision displeased my parents, who were not comfortable with the foreign religion. And indeed, it was this choice of religion, Western religion, and of its deeper commitments, that most upset my family and occasioned the conflicts of my youth and early adulthood. Later on, it was also this reli-

---

6. C. G. Jung, *Memories, Dreams, Reflections* (New York: Pantheon Books, 1973), 44–45.

7. While celebrated in poetry, Mulan's story is not well documented in history. We are not even sure of her real surname, her dates, and place of origin. Presumed to hail from northern China, she is variously said to be from the late fifth century A.D. or some other time.

gious choice that made me feel different from most of my fellow countrymen, that also complicated very much my consciousness as well as my conscience. In looking back, I am not always sure this has been worth it, even if I must admit that this initial decision to become a Catholic has shaped much of my life and my identity. Among other things, it has given me the tension of multiple identities and conflicting loyalties, to traditions, cultures, and values.

Having Multiple Identities

Living in any society, there are some of us who feel more potentially divided than others. In sociological language, we may have "selves that are more difficult to organize," whether as native or black; as Asian Americans or French Canadians or, much worse, as Sudanese Christians or Serbo-Croatian Muslims. Indeed, belonging to "two worlds," or, if we prefer to call it, "many worlds," is so difficult that countries are being torn apart in the name of a simpler identity, whether that be ethnic or linguistic or religious.

It is not easy to belong to two worlds, and harder still to live in both at the same time. Certain things are obvious: as an Asian woman living in North America, I am very conscious of my Asian background. I teach Asian culture and Asian values, while living in a society where the hidden norm is still white Anglo-Saxon Protestant, and of course, male.

Dualities often lead to experience of powerlessness and victimization. But dualities may also lead to larger cultural space and greater opportunities, if such are recognized. But then, if we also want deeper personal satisfaction, this usually comes at a price: it has to be earned, and the earning may be a lifelong struggle.

Poised between East and West, I am puzzled by the contrast often made of West and East, that somehow, the Western mind is marked by a greater rationality than the Eastern. Certainly, in things religious, the Easterner finds the believer in the West affirming so much that goes against reason, in doctrines of theology like the Trinity, the Incarnation, the Resurrection, even if the language of theology tends to be a rational one. In the Orient, it is less religion, and more spirituality, that is valued, because it is closer to experience and more relevant to life. The language of spirituality may often appear intuitive, but it is usually not opposed to reason; rather, it is based on insight derived from experience.[8]

I have also been impressed by the differing priorities given to religious belief and to spiritual experience. A frequent criticism directed by Western Christians, especially missionaries, against Chinese civilization is that it lacked the dimension of transcendence. By that, they mean that it lacked a clear belief in a Supreme deity. And this belief is posited as virtually self-evident, since, after all, "The fool hath said in his heart, 'There is no God' " (Ps. 14:1; Ps. 53:1). But the Easterner asserts that transcendence may be discerned in its immanence, especially in the lives of those sage figures who radiate wisdom and compassion. These same figures, however, are often respectfully ignorant of divinity, because it is conceit to assert that there is certainly a God whom one can never see.

Historically, an interesting point of convergence between Western Christianity and Eastern devotion has been the place of the feminine in popular piety. Within the Catholic tradition, the cult of Mary, the mother of Jesus, bears striking similarity to the Buddhist cult to Kuan-yin, the so-called goddess of mercy. While I am mostly supportive of the reforms of Vatican Council II, I regret the loss in status suffered by Mary in recent years. I do not desire her deification, but I feel that Mary not only represents womanhood and motherhood in religion, but serves also as a model for contemplation, as someone who kept many things to herself, "pondering over them in her heart" (Luke 2:51). Without her, the Christian religion becomes too masculine, often iconoclastic. When one comes to think of it, Chinese Buddhism had to invent a female figure in the Bodhisattva Kuan-yin, originally venerated in a male form, in response to popular need for a protectress, one not a mother herself, but who listens and responds effectively to the prayers of would-be mothers.

---

8. Here, the East refers usually to the Far East, that is, East Asia, while the West refers to Western Europe and North America.

There is also the contrast over the teacher figure. For the West, a prophet is the bearer of God's message, respected because this is from God, rather than for its inherent truth. But of course, one needs first to believe in God before one can accept his messenger. And then, flowing from this prophet ideal, a Western theologian, while a teacher of religion, is often not much different from the teachers of chemistry or computer science. And a Western philosopher would be insulted should we suggest that he or she is imparting wisdom rather than skills in critical thinking. He or she is required to be competent, but not necessarily to be God-like or wise. On the contrary, the Easterner who is a spiritual leader is something of a sage, someone who gives of his own insights, someone who himself (usually a man) incorporates those spiritual ideals that he also teaches.

Once more, Carl Jung has observed:

> To Western man, the meaninglessness of a merely static universe is unbearable. He must assume that it has meaning. The Oriental does not need to make this assumption; rather, he himself embodies it. . . .
>
> I would say that both are right. Western man seems predominantly extroverted, Eastern man predominantly introverted. The former projects the meaning and considers that it exists in objects; the latter feels the meaning in himself. But the meaning is both without and within.[9]

Living in the West, I have become accustomed to thinking of myself as being not-someone else, if only because this is the way others understand me. I am nonwhite and nonmale. I come from a non-Christian family, and have little to say to most people who go to church or preach in it. And while I find the earlier Latin Catholic services too formal and structured, I find the more recent varieties somewhat casual and not helpful to contemplation. In my own life, I am very active. When I go to church, I long for silence, but usually endure chatter.

And then, when I travel to China, I wonder whether the culture and values to which I am still attached are already defunct

---

9. Jung, *Memories, Dreams, Reflections,* 317.

there, or perhaps exist only in my romanticized imagination. For even there, I define myself by saying what I am not: not a local, not a Communist, not a citizen of China. And yet, I am always identified as Chinese, in both North America and in Europe. I guess I have a perpetual identity crisis.

Joseph Kitagawa, formerly dean of Chicago Divinity School, has expressed very well his own dilemma, which is, in many ways, mine too:

> An Easterner coming to settle in the West faces a number of alternatives. He can consciously remain an Easterner and try to interpret Eastern religions from this perspective. Or he can identify himself with the West and study Eastern religions as a Westerner...insofar as his method [is] ...concerned. Or again, he can choose to stand in a borderland, being conscious of...both sides but...refusing to be drawn into either side.... [I have] chosen still another alternative, and a more difficult one...to identify [myself] ...with the West without losing [my identity]...with the East.[10]

I recognize my own choice in his choice. I do not find the values and cultures of either East or West entirely satisfying, but I find enough in each culture that is worth appreciating, and also worth criticizing. I find that such an alternative — to be both Eastern and Western — is possible, because, in spite of the differences, and even the contradictions, there is sufficient common ground between East and West. And this common ground is that which makes all of us human. The values to which I am attached are after all, human values, with all their potential for conflict. The community in which I live and work is, after all, a human community, with all its latent and manifest tensions.

Besides, if we all reflect more deeply on the subject, we would realize that, in a sense, it is our common lot, no matter who we are and where we are — to belong to, and to live in, different worlds. I am, of course, speaking of various levels of *duality*

---

10. Joseph M. Kitagawa, *Religions of the East* (Philadelphia: Westminster Press, 1968), Foreword, 12.

within the one identity. The levels include the outer, sociological, as well as the inner, psychological. We are all conscious of ourselves as selves, and of others as nonselves. In our behavior, we usually have to take into account the feelings and expectations of others, whether we like these or not.

When we turn inward, we become conscious of the actual/potential split within: what we are as opposed to what we would like to be. As in the case of Chuang Tzu, we might also muse over the choice of a butterfly in a dream as his *alter ego:* "a butterfly flitting and fluttering around, happy with himself and doing as he pleased."

The image of the butterfly is here one of freedom and happiness, even if we recognize in the butterfly itself a creature whose very appearance bespeaks a hold on life that is evanescent. This is a contrast with the "solid and unmistakable Chuang Chou," a recluse who meditated on the sufferings around him, whether they be disease or death, or war, poverty, and injustice. There are many ways of interpreting him. One way is to regard him as having much to say in protest against the society of his own times, while longing for greater happiness and freedom. Here, as someone imbued with the moral principles of both Christianity and Confucianism, I might add: this is a man with a personal as well as a social identity, with all the cares and responsibilities these bring him, even if he was living in semiretirement. In that sense, many of us could identify with Chuang Tzu, wishing perhaps that he was the butterfly, even if that means embracing the insecurity of evanescence.

The Threats to Identity

> Man's life is but a jest,
> A dream, a shadow, bubble, air, a vapor at the best.[11]

Is life but a dream? Even if we do not wish to accept this, we cannot but feel at times the fragility of it all. And, a person's identity

---

11. George Walter Thornbury, *The Jester's Sermon*; see *A Second Treasury of the Familiar,* ed. Ralph L. Woods (New York: Macmillan, 1950), 629.

is as fragile as the person who claims it. There are many potential threats to identity, of which the worst is the threat to life and health. For

> Only in ill health does one realize the intricacy of the body; and only in a crisis, individual or historical, does it become obvious what a sensitive combination of interrelated factors the human personality is.[12]

With many people, this awareness of being "doomed to death" may continue for a painfully long time, presumably a reason why Martin Heidegger has spoken about *Zum Tode Sein* or Being-toward-death:

> Dasein, as thrown Being-in-the-world, ... has in every case already been delivered over to its death. In being towards its death, Dasein is dying factically and indeed constantly, as long as it has not yet come to its demise.[13]

For Heidegger, the answer is to consider death without flinching as a horizon of life rather than as its annihilation. The existentialist theologian Paul Tillich would call such an attitude *The Courage to Be*. Nevertheless, he was careful to warn against any pseudocourage that is rooted in escape from reality and from the affirmation of self:

> Much courage to be, created by religion, is nothing else than the desire to limit one's own being and to strengthen this limitation through the power of religion ... [reducing] the openness of man ... to the reality which is himself.[14]

We have to live with the awareness of such threats to the very ground of our identity. Most recently, it has led to a whole society's quest to exclude from its conscious mind everything that may represent death. But long before that, it might also have launched some people into inquiries concerning what follows this life. And we know some of the answers that have been proposed.

---

12. Erikson, *Young Man Luther*, 14.

13. Martin Heidegger, *Being and Time*, trans. John Macquarrie and Edward Robinson (New York: Harper & Row, 1962), 303.

14. Paul Tillich, *The Courage to Be* (New Haven: Yale University Press, 1952), 73.

There are those who assert this life is just one ring in a chain of many lives or existences of what is called samsara. Those believers in this theory who are not Buddhists have the consolation that personal survival is assured, although the form of existence may change. There are others who assert that this life will be followed by a qualitatively better life, in a change of state called resurrection, when one is taken into the embrace of the Godhead. The believers in this theory include today Jews, Christians, and Muslims. They can take consolation in the thought that the survival of their identity is assured, albeit in a transformed state. Such theories serve to give meaning to life, and with it, to one's identity. They are answers to the question, "What for? Why am I what I am? Is there a purpose behind all this?"

Several times in my life, I have been seriously sick. Metaphorically speaking, I know what it means to look down into the abyss that may mean nothingness. Of course I realize that we are all mortal. And, with this realization, I cannot help but wonder sometimes what it all means — this identity, this unity with oneself, this belonging to a network of relationships with other identities, together with all that accompanied the building of this unity, when one day, it will all be taken away.

Chuang Tzu speaks often of dreams, and of the difficulty of distinguishing a dream state from a state of awakened consciousness:

> While [a man]...is dreaming he does not know it is a dream, and in his dream he may even try to interpret a dream. Only after he wakes does he know it was a dream.[15]

I am, indeed, very conscious of the rhythm and contrast of day and night, of awaking and of sleeping, perhaps dreaming. In the daytime, I seek to affirm and assert my various identities, struggling to give them an overall unity. I have an active temperament. I live and work as a Westerner, even if my subject happens to be Eastern religion. My reason is usually in control.

At night, the situation is different. My reason is much less in control, as memories of the past, accompanied by repressed emo-

---

15. Watson, *The Complete Works of Chuang Tzu*, 47

tions, dominate my subconsciousness. When I do sleep, I often have difficult and intense dreams, in which I find myself in roles very different from those of the daytime. It is as if the conflicts of my multiple identities are coming back to haunt me. And I long for silence and contemplation, even in my dream state.

Without doubt, the dream often indicates a suppressed desire or an unresolved conflict, either of which might be related to certain threats to our personal identity. It takes wisdom to learn how to interpret and respond to one's dreams, since this is part and parcel of the whole of reality.

There are, however, other threats to personal identity which regard free will and choice. The deeper ones usually involve our very survival, as we ponder the options of transcending self-attachment in the name of a greater good. In the words of the Chinese sage Mencius, who uses the analogy of food choices:

> Fish is what I want; bear's paw is also what I want. If I cannot have both, I would rather have bear's paw than fish. Life is what I want; virtue is also what I want. If I cannot have both, I would rather have virtue than life. For while I want life, I also want something more than life.... And while I loathe death, I also loathe something worse than death.[16]

Presumably, if life was not dear, giving it up would not only be easy, it would also be less costly. So we should not be surprised that the very brave are often those who feel themselves the most cowardly, as they confront their finitude. The Protestant theologian Dietrich Bonhoeffer (1906–45), while a prisoner in Nazi Germany, has given expression of his own inner struggle in a poem:

> Who am I? This or the Other?
> Am I one person today and tomorrow another?
> Am I both at once? A hypocrite before others,
> and before myself a contemptible woebegone weakling?
> Or is something within me still like a beaten army

---

16. Mencius VIA: 10. The English translation is my own. Bear's paw remains a delicacy served in certain restaurants in the Orient, to the dismay of many lovers of wildlife.

fleeing in disorder from victory already achieved?
Who am I? They mock me, these lonely questions of mine.[17]

A Common Identity

Few of us may be called to make a voluntary self-sacrifice as was
Dietrich Bonhoeffer. Safely removed now from the naive idealism
of my youth, I am happy today that I did not have to be a Chinese
Joan of Arc. Besides, with all my admiration for Bonhoeffer, I
find it difficult to accept with childlike simplicity his final line:

Whoever I am, Thou knowest, O God, I am thine![18]

To me, the word *God* is much more complicated than it is to
him. I think of it first in English, and then in Chinese...and I
get a little confused. What does the word God mean? Is it the
same as the Chinese word for spirit, *shen* (Japanese: *kami*), or is
it rather the ever old and ever new Lord-on-high (*Shang-ti*), as
the Chinese Protestants still call him, or perhaps we should only
call him, as do Chinese Catholics, Lord of Heaven (*T'ien-chu*)?[19]
Is this God strictly personal, or a God "beyond theism," to use
the words of Paul Tillich?[20]

Once more, I derive some consolation from Chuang Tzu's
playful imagination:

How do I know that loving life is not a delusion? How do I
know that in hating death I am not like a man who, having
left home in his youth, has forgotten the way back?[21]

---

17. This is quoted in Gerhard Leibholz's memoir, in Dietrich Bonhoeffer, *The
Cost of Discipleship*, rev. ed. (New York: Macmillan, 1959), 15. The English
translation of the poem is by J. B. Leishman.

18. Ibid.

19. I am referring here to the common practice today for Chinese Catholics and
Protestants to address God in different terms, either as Lord of Heaven, or as Lord-
on-high. This goes back to the controversy over translation of terms which occurred
in the seventeenth and eighteenth centuries. But the practice continues to make
Catholics and Protestants appear as if they belong to different religions.

20. One problem for regarding God as personal is linguistic. The Chinese term
for *personal* includes the words *jen-ko*, which basically implies anthropomorphic
character.

21. Watson, *The Complete Works of Chuang Tzu*, 47.

The confusion, however, is only on the intellectual plane. Existentially, I live and pray as a believer in a God whom I presume to be good and loving. But even my manner of praying is an "East-West" encounter. Since a recent illness, I have returned to regular meditation, which I do somewhat in a Taoist or Zen fashion. I don't meditate long enough or seriously enough. But I do try to meditate every day. At the beginning of each session, I am very conscious of the fears and anxieties that accompany my self-consciousness; I am also somewhat conscious of those others with whom I share my small world. But as I direct my intention to a higher presence, while forgetting my self and its ordinary anxieties, I derive a greater sense of inner peace.

Nevertheless, fears and anxieties usually return with self-consciousness, as the sense of peace subsides. The inner life has its own demons, sometimes worse than those of the outer life. And it has been said that the "mystical courage to be lasts as long as the mystical situation":[22]

> Its limit is the state of emptiness of being and meaning, with its horror and despair, which the mystics have described. . . .
> To experience this and to endure it is the courage to be of the mystic in the state of emptiness. . . .
>
> Since everything that is participates in the power of being, the element of identity on which mysticism is based cannot be absent in any religious experience.[23]

So what is identity after all? It is so much part of our very self, and yet, it is only in forgetting this very self, that we may find oneness with the self. In those moments of silence, I lose my identity crisis, because I find my deeper identity. I forget who I am. And yet, I am very much at one with those others who may rub against me, or be rubbed against by me. In spite of all differences, we share a common identity in the human community.

I know that I shall have to live with many of my conflicts and uncertainties, rather than expect to resolve them. For years, I thought that a wise guide could help. With maturity, I realize

---

22. Tillich, *The Courage to Be*, 159.
23. Ibid., 159–60.

that there is no other who can resolve them for me. In fact, I think that living with conflicts, and seeking to go beyond them, is itself a manner of resolving them, perhaps the only way, of resolving them.

> The courage to take the anxiety of meaninglessness upon oneself is the boundary line up to which the courage to be can go. Beyond it is mere non-being. Within it all forms of courage are re-established in the power of the God above the God of theism. The courage to be is rooted in the God who appears when God has disappeared in the anxiety of doubt.[24]

Life is more than a dream, because in life, we experience both the dream state and the state of awakening. But if the dream can be a symbol for the ambiguity of life, so the awakening can be a symbol for the clarity that we hope lies beyond. As Chuang Tzu has mused, at the end of his story about the dream in which he was the butterfly: "And someday there will be a great awakening when we know that this is all a great dream."[25]

24. Tillich, *The Courage to Be*, 190.
25. Watson, *The Complete Works of Chuang Tzu*, 47.

Chapter 2

Religious Identity and Pluralism

Raimon Panikkar

The Claim of Our Times

The Past Hundred Years

The Chicago Centenary of the World Parliament of Religions is not only a commemoration of the past, it is also a celebration of the present and a challenge for the future. The three times are all involved. We are at a crucial moment. During the past hundred years a giant step has been made, mainly by the academic community. Gone, by and large, are the days of distrust and exclusivism. We know and respect each other. We have to confess that the intellectual world has been doing a pioneering work.

But the world externally (politically, economically, socially . . .) has not improved much. Religious institutions are still lagging behind the challenges of our time. Religious warfare and violence are rampant all over the world. We could give examples in the five continents.

Could it be that the religious "parliaments" have been only that: parliaments and not actions? Could it be that the lack of action is due to a lack of contemplation? This should be a warning to us. Perhaps religions themselves need conversion, *metanoia*.

Could it be that we treat religions as mere sociological constructs and have developed a nonreligious notion of religion? Influenced perhaps by the scientific ideology, or by the political arenas, have we not forgotten that religions are more —

23

not less — than sets of doctrines or gatherings of peoples? Or
that we see only the good side of religion and are blind to its
shadows?

Is it a lack of the mystical dimension? Perhaps we should fall
prostrate on the ground, remain silent — and get up only to go
out to the streets and places of the world once filled with the
power of the Spirit.

•

This is not a preamble, but the core of my discourse.

As it has to be a dis-course, I shall follow the course of words.

A parliament of religions, truthful to its name, should be a
parliament, that is, a *parable* of religions: a "putting side by
side" (*paraballein*) the different religions of the world, not as in
a supermarket for sale, but in an agora, an assembly for mutual
knowledge, stimulation, enrichment up to a possible reciprocal
fecundation, and action flowing from the new insights. We should
come out with a new and authentic parable.

When the religious traditions of humankind began to come
into a more intimate and wider contact than through skirmishes
on the battlefields or in casual encounters, a new situation began to develop: the religion of our neighbor, who lives no longer
beyond the mountains or overseas but just around the corner
or in the next house, begins to present an unavoidable question both for dealing with the neighbor and for dealing with my
own religion, too. We can hardly avoid comparing, judging, and
eventually deciding.

I detect three types of reactions. I would contest all of them.

a. *The aggressive attitude.* Our religion is better, superior, ultimately the only one way of living a truly human life leading to
perfection and "salvation." The brutal word today is *exclusivism.*

But there is another milder word. It is *evolutionism.* The other
religions are not exactly wrong, but they are religions "on the
way to development" as the self-appointed "First World" still of-
ficially calls the other two-thirds of humanity. The other religions
would then be not altogether false, but on their way to reaching "our" stage of development. We stand at the head of a linear

evolution, from the religion of the *Pithecanthropus erectus* up to our brand.

Theologians will explain it, obviously, with a fascinating array of words: We are all realized souls, but we (or rather the others) don't know it; we all belong to the invisible *umma*, church (although only we, unlike the others, of course, know the visible one); we are all the same; the masses quarrel for trifles, but we belong to the few who know it; there is one God for all, but it goes without saying that ours is the best conception of that God; we are all sinners, but only we know how to repent.

Western christianity, that magnificent blend of european spirit and hebrew inspiration, offers a masterpiece example of this "fulfillment theology."

b. *The regressive attitude.* All religions are just operating on some archaic levels of consciousness, and they express themselves in diverse languages and universes of discourse. Divergences are accidental, and ultimately the very core is also an illusion. Religion is vitally and virtually obsolete. The brutal word is *indifferentism*.

The milder word is *tolerance*. We tolerate religions because they are neither powerful nor important enough to upset our accepted or imposed status quo. In the last analysis the religion of my neighbor is not threatening because my own religion is not challenging either. Religion becomes secondary and sinks into a private devotion without any relevance for at least public life. "Parliament of Religions"? Let them talk! Probably the participants have nothing better to do. Meanwhile we run the world on other lines. Another healthy warning for some. We can all agree to disagree because ultimately it does not matter.

c. *The progressive attitude.* We have learned by now that there is no absolute truth, that truth is scattered on all sides and in all religions so that we pick up our own brand, make up our minds, decide our choices, and produce an eclectic mix which satisfies our needs and allows us to be respectful of others, and feel somewhat superior to those fundamentalists of all sorts and indifferences of all types — of the two previous attitudes.

Some people may call this third reaction the "pluralistic" religion needed for a "pluralistic" culture like ours. Not without a major reason this parliament has put the problem of pluralism as the first item of the "major presentations."

Nobody has the monopoly on words, but for the same reason one is free to use them, provided one describes sufficiently the meaning ascribed to them.

I submit that the word *pluralism*, as I have been using it for over a quarter of a century, is susceptible of denoting and connoting another semantic field different from the exclusivistic, the indifferent, and the eclectic.

I shall maintain that there is no pluralistic religion, but that there is a pluralistic attitude toward religions. The question touches the very foundations of our dominant culture and brings us to the brink of the indispensable mutation of our times. The very meaning of religion is here put into question. Religions cannot "save" the individual by extricating the individual from humanity. They cannot "save" humanity by severing human beings from the earth.

But before elaborating on this, I should clarify a couple of points.

Role and Danger of Labels

I have criticized eclecticism, understood as a cocktail of bits and pieces of different religions. But the alternative is neither stagnant immovability nor what I would call the tyranny of labels.

To put names to things and events is a human prerogative. But naming means much more than putting labels on things. This latter activity belongs to a secondary role of the mind: the calculus. This quantification has gained the upper hand in some cultures and has led to what I have called classificatory mania, of which modern science offers us the supreme example. If you detect a different atomic weight in an atom which should be of hydrogen because it occupies its place in the periodic table of elements (of Mendeleyev) you will give it another name, and call it a hydrogen isotope and clearly distinguish deuterium from hydrogen. We put a label on a particular acid, write H_2SO_4, and call it sulfuric acid. If we find a somewhat similar but weaker acid, because it has an atom less of oxygen (H_2SO_3), we call it sulfurous acid. Labels are univocal. They have only a single referent.

Names have a much larger flexibility. They are polysemic. A certain way of life and set of beliefs of a group of jews and greeks at Antioch some two thousand years ago was named christianity. What we call today by the same name has enormously increased in atomic and even molecular weight, but we go on calling it by the same name. Sometimes we put on them different sublabels like roman, greek, protestant, and anglican, but we cannot put individual labels on all christians. The classification would fail its purpose. Christianity denotes only a certain family resemblance, but this likeness is today no longer univocal. Often the similarities cross family lines: there may be more likeness between a protestant and a catholic activist than between a roman catholic fundamentalist and a liberal one.

Labels themselves need to be changed today. The very label "religion" needs transformation. Our present-day categories are becoming more and more obsolete.

The Present Situation

How far can words stretch their meaning? Or, to come to our question, how far can we keep our religious identity and be open to a pluralistic attitude? In order to be pluralistic, do we have to renounce our religious affiliations, our particular beliefs and endorse only a general religiosity common to all traditions?

This is our problem: *pluralism and religious identity.*

This question is neither rhetorical nor merely academic. It has a vital importance, especially today. Religious identity has direct repercussions for ethnic, political, and national identity. The black american in the United States, the happenings in Northern Ireland, in the Balkan Peninsula, and in India, are all burning examples that religious identity cannot be treated lightly and irresponsibly. Do religions accept that the world needs thirty million soldiers and employs 60 percent of its resources for war? Can religion be blind to the fact that 20 percent of humanity consumes, manages, and "enjoys" 85 percent of all sources of energy? That a country like Thailand can subsist thanks to prostitution and Colombia and Bolivia mainly to the cultivation of drugs? When the world is burning, how can religions bypass such issues.

The present-day problem is an ultimate question of life and death. Is this not a religious issue?

Pluralism

The Alleged Dangers of Pluralism

Before describing how I understand pluralism, let me dramatize not a straw man but the actual situation of a majority of religious people.

Are you going to Chicago? You must be very rich to begin with, have much leisure time to talk about religion and little time to practice your own concrete, limited, but real religion.

Are you there going to vote, like in a parliament, in order to find where religious truth lies? Are you going to decide by majority? Are you going to discard, for the sake of human understanding, all reference to a Supreme Being, who might have decided that there be not only cows, roses, and rocks but also elected people, bearers of divine revelation and responsible ones for the divine decrees? The cow does not feel it to be a divine injustice that she is not a flower, nor a jew or a parsi feel superior or inferior because she belongs to a minority religion.

What are the rules of the game of your parliament? A profane house of palaver daring to deal with sacred things? An egalitarian agora in which the atheist, the animist, the believers in a divine revelation and those who abhor even the notion of it are going to be put on the same level, disregarding human history and divine reality? You are not discussing political rights or contesting a certain human equal dignity. You are supposed to discuss religious rights and try to do religious justice to both those who do not accept any particular theistic interference in human affairs and those who firmly believe that a theistic factor is a decisive element in any sensible talk about reality. How can they be brought together without betraying one of them?

Is a democratic arena the appropriate instrument to deal with theocratic realities? Or is pluralism the stratagem to induce people to give up their own identities in order to create a new world order in which all cats are gray, all differences abolished under the pretext of tolerance and peace?

Thus speaks the *pûrvapakshin;* thus runs the objection. In short, does pluralism threaten our religious identity? Is it a betrayal of religion, an abandonment of the rights of truth?

Some Definitions

In the context of our problem we could understand *tradition* as that which provides the background for our cultural identity; and *religion* as that which offers our own ultimate identity. This is possible only within a tradition. Tradition and religion are not synonymous, but they are intimately connected. The ultimate contents of a tradition are formed by its religious core. Religion gives each culture its ultimate content and culture each religion its language — without specifying further at this time.

Pluralism, as I have elaborated time and again, is the utmost effort to deal with diversity without abandoning rationality. It is the outcome of the realistic and mature reaction of the intellect which, after having assimilated the cumulative human experience of the last six to eight thousand years, comes to the insight that the empirical multiplicity of things can neither be reduced to intellectual unity nor left alone in an unrelated plurality: *diversitatis splendor.*

Indeed, the apparent multiplicity of entities is reduced to intelligible unity in the concept or the idea. It is the problem of universals. But, unless we put all the ontic weight on the idea, relegating things to mere appearances, that is, unless we subscribe to a radical monism, we have to acknowledge that the concept, or formal structure of a thing, is a mental abstraction which has left a portion of reality out of the picture. Whatever degree of reality the idea may have, it is not the entire reality. There are many things green, but the color green is a mere concept that is not exhausted in a single green thing. Or, to avoid unnecessary problems for ourselves, we may put forth the second-degree example of the many colors. But color is not a color; it has no color. Green or blue is a color. Color is only an abstraction, a generalization, a common denominator or a common character to all colors.

We cannot combine all colors in one supercolor. We recognize colors and we may have a concept of color, but color does not exist. There is only the concept of color. Some would say that color denotes the essence of color, but this alleged essence of color, realized as it may be in green or blue, is still not identical to green or blue.

There may be an essence of religion. I doubt it, for other reasons, but we may assume it for the sake of argument. Yet, islam is not identical with the essence of religion. Islam is a particular way of realizing this essence that is different from the way in which taoism "realizes" this allegedly same essence. The rites, doctrines, and moods of these two religions are different, mutually incompatible. The mere concept of religion does not cover all that islam or taoism is.

Pluralism between Monism and Dualism

I make three statements.

a. *Pluralism is not sheer plurality.* This is a fact. There are many colors. They are irreducible to each other. If we want to embrace them together we cannot do it in an intelligible way without reducing colors to color. The notion of color is an abstraction, a formal concept, a universal, but not identical to the thing. The real thing is a concrete particular color.

There are also many religions. "Let a thousand flowers bloom!" This is not pluralism. Religions are not like flowers because some religions claim to occupy the entire earth, making impossible the blossoming of other religions; they want to grow in such a way as to choke out all the other neighboring flowers. Religions are not like flowers either because some doctrinal or moral contents of religion may appear not just as different as a rose and a tulip, but contradictory as a flower and a nonflower. Pluralism emerges when multiplicity becomes an intellectual and an existential problem, when contradiction becomes acute or coexistence seems impossible.

Plurality refers to objects; it is the multiplicity of objects which we perceive in one way or another. It is normally a quantifiable concept. It belongs to objectivity.

Pluralism, on the contrary, is not primarily objective. It does not say anything directly about objects. Certainly, it is based on the perception of plurality, but it includes also a subjective attitude. It bounces back to the knowing subject and discovers the inherent limitations of the very process of intelligibility. Pluralism rebounds on the subject, as it were, once the subject has struck a radical incomprehensibility, once we face mutually incompatible statements which defy any dialectical *Aufhebung*. Instead of getting stuck in the objective impasse, we examine whether the cause may not lie on our side, on the side of the knowing subject, ultimately in the very act of knowing and the nature of knowledge itself. Nothing warrants that knowledge is the ultimate criterion of all reality, except that we do not have any other. Knowledge is the ultimate criterion of truth by the very definition of truth as appertaining to the knowing act. But our criteria purport to be criteria of reality and not only of intelligibility. Now, without jumping outside rationality, we can be aware that this rationality is limited by its own assumption, namely, that knowledge is the criterion of the real. But this does not guarantee that the field of the real is identical with the intelligible — that the sphere of Being coalesces with that of Thinking.

b. *Pluralism is irreducible to unity — even of a higher order.* The many colors of our empirical world are subsumed into an abstract idea of color which belongs to a higher degree of abstraction and thus to a lower degree of reality. Pluralism is not structuralism or formalism of any kind. Indeed, if we speak of religions in the plural it is because the singular has a certain meaning. But this meaning can be only formal. What entitles us to put confucianism and judaism under the same concept? Or even Marxism and scientism? Multiplicity is only of homogeneous entities like colors. We speak of pluralism when plurality is not reducible to an intelligible multiplicity, that is, when there is something which defies classification into a set of units; something different from mere unity and something different from multiplicity. Pluralism does not amount to saying that there are "many colors," because the "many" has meaning only if we know what is color. Pluralism does not amount to saying that there is color, because this "one" color does not exist. Pluralism is a realistic attitude which, having realized the irreducibility of multiplicity to unity, tries to embrace the whole without reducing it to the quantifiable sum total of its parts or to a formal unity of whatever type.

c. *Pluralism stands between unity and plurality — without dialectically oscillating between them.* Dialectics is a genial effort at not abandoning rationalism. It is the momentous outcome of Hegel in modern times, be it of the idealistic or materialistic type. Pluralism, on the other hand, abandons rationalism, but not rationality. It overcomes rationalism without abdicating in favor of irrationalism. It is the rational effort which leads us to discover intellectually the very limits of reason, because of the factual impossibility of reducing everything to unity (i.e., to intelligibility), without for that matter falling into the opposite extreme of chaotic irrationality.

Pluralism differs from the pragmatic *epochê*, the suspension of judgment waiting for an eschatological solution postponing rational decisions until the end of times or to an indefinite future. If we have to maintain rationality in human behavior, decisions cannot be indefinitely postponed. God does not play dice, said Einstein. But God may play with more than one set of rules, which gives us the impression of sheer randomness. Pluralism maintains rationality.

Therefore, pluralism is not a supersystem. Nobody can follow a supposedly pluralistic system without infringing upon rationality and the principle of noncontradiction. I cannot adhere to a belief system in which God both creates and does not create the world. In fact, such a system (*systêma*) does not exist. Pluralism is an attitude which emerges when we acknowledge the limits of reason and do not identify them with the limits of Being; when we do not equate Thinking and Being, to speak against Parmenides, or assume a priori the total intelligibility of reality. In other words, the conviction of pluralism dawns upon the human mind when we discover our own contingency, our own intellectual limitations, and do not compensate our impotence by projecting our frustration onto an infinite Mind which will reassure us that our ignorance is only ours — and for the time being. The existence of an infinite mind is not called into question here. What is called into question is the identification of this infinite mind with the entire reality. An omniscient mind will know all that is knowable, but all that is knowable does not need to be all that *is*, unless we gratuitously postulate the total intelligibility of reality.

After the triple failure witnessed by over six thousand years of human experience we may be prone to consider the rationality and plausibility of the pluralistic attitude. These are the failures:

The historico-political failure of creating peace on earth should make us think very seriously whether the parmenidian scheme, with all its variations, is the only paradigm of rationality. The philosophico-dialectical failure of reducing into a single scheme of intelligibility incompatible worldviews and philosophies cannot be easily whisked away by saying that we are smarter than all our predecessors and shall now overcome all the aporias — with a "universal theology (or philosophy) of religion." The religio-cultural failure of humanity should equally prevent us from falling into the uncritical naïveté that our Parliament of Religions, or any other one, will reduce all religions to a single religion — in which we shall live happily hereafter. Pluralism dawns when we experience the relativity (not relativism) of all our concepts, insights, and convictions — and of our human condition as such.

The pluralistic attitude is the fruit of a long genesis: We recognize mutually incompatible styles of life and contradictory doctrines. We are at the same time convinced of the goodness of our own lifestyle and the truth of our doctrines. And yet, the different positions are mutually irreducible, and, being ultimate, we cannot accept a dialectical *Aufhebung*. It all boils down to confessing that we sincerely believe that the other is wrong, and even sometimes evil, although we may have to tolerate the other. All efforts at unity have failed, and this failure has lasted for thousands of years. It is high time that we cease to cherish the idea that we are going to succeed in the "war that shall end all wars."

The pluralistic attitude simply takes away the sting of absolutism on both sides, precisely because we have experienced that we are limited and not absolute. We shall try by all legitimate means to overpower or convince the other, but because we are not absolute bearers of absolute values (on either side) there is still room for a possible common field, a common arena where we may encounter ourselves if we insist and persist in finding one. In short, we shall never "break relations" — even if this be only from the part of the pluralist.

Pluralists do not give up personal convictions. They simply do not absolutize them. There is not only the benefit of the doubt. There is also the credit of the other. Even those who claim to speak in the Name of God cannot avoid speaking in their own name and in their own tongue. The *ab-solutus* would literally be invisible, inaudible, unspeakable, *solutus* from everything.

Pluralism amounts to the critical acknowledgment of the human condition; and religious pluralism to the confession that we are not the Absolute.

Pluralism does not necessarily affirm that there are many true religions. This may be how christians fear, burdened as they are with the old idea of having the only true religion. Pluralism does not affirm that there are many truths — which is a contradiction in terms. Truth is itself pluralistic, not plural; that is, it is related to the context from which it comes and to the people for whom it is (appears, is revealed as) truth.

Pluralism simply acknowledges that there are belief systems, worldviews, philosophies, or religions that are mutually incommensurable. It encourages, further, the establishment of bilateral pacts — dialogue between two such systems so that in the dialogue itself we may work out the procedure and the contents of the encounter.

This is more than the discovery of the other. The other is all too often the "other" version of the self, its complement, even its critique, but ultimately its creation. The "other" is all too easily assimilated into our own parameters of understanding. The other of pluralism is not our *other* but another "self," irreducible to our self, and to the "other" of our selfsame self.

Is there any type of possible relationship outside that of the other?

Yes. This is the thou, which only love discovers: a *thou* which demands reciprocity. The dialogue leads to the discovery of the thou which appears when my self submits to being questioned by another self. The thou is neither the self nor the nonself.

Religious Identity

The Question

Our original question was this: Can we keep our religious identity and maintain a pluralistic attitude? Are we not betraying or at least diluting our respective religious traditions if we subscribe to pluralism? We are not questioning whether we all should be tolerant, receptive, sympathetic, and even open to other religions. We take this for granted. We are asking whether such tolerance, sympathy, and openness do not have their foundation precisely in pluralism. Otherwise, there is the danger that our tolerance is only a move to neutralize the other, our sympathy a show to hide our disapproval, our openness a strategy to profit from the relationship and so bring the "miscarried" to our fold.

My thesis should be clear by now. The historical step of this Parliament of Religions could be the endorsement, obviously pluralistic, of religious pluralism. By doing this we do not pass objective judgment on religions; we pass judgment on ourselves and our way of dealing with other religions.

After so many millennia of human historical experience we should be prepared to question whether the old religious paradigms are sufficient. They may still be necessary, but perhaps no longer sufficient. In the last hundred years, and in the minds and hearts of many enlightened people for thousands of years, humanity has become painfully aware that without religious peace, wholehearted tolerance, mutual religious respect, and sincere openness to the other we cannot survive as a human race, nor can the individual lead a truly human existence. I submit that without this acknowledgment of pluralism all those beautiful ideals are stripped of their foundation and become only manipulable pseudovalues in the hands of the powerful. Pluralism offers the intellectual basis for such attitudes.

There is but one snag: Do we not betray our religious beliefs? Is not the price to be paid for pluralism a betrayal of the very core of each religion, as I have already hinted at? Would not the remedy be worse than the malady? Should we not rather content ourselves with a pragmatic liberal "laissez-faire" and expect enough common sense so as to opt for the lesser evil? Pluralism

lies at the heart of an excruciating moral question. Why shouldn't
we start a crusade if (we believe that) the other is evil? The rights
of God stand above the rights of human beings. The *dharma* does
not accept a compromise with *adharma*. Truth cannot yield to
untruth. Is pluralism not going to undermine our zeal for justice
and truth? Where do we stand if we abandon all our convictions?

I shall let the religious answer be preceded by a philosophical
commentary.

Personal Identity

What is the meaning of religious identity? We shall not linger
now on the debated questions of whether there is a permanent
self, or whether the personal identity is just a question of our
body, our memory, or touch upon the vexed problem of the
substance along with the aporias of change and permanence.

I shall make only two observations concerning the very nature
of our human thinking.

The first says simply this. It is in the very nature of our human
intellect to seek to reduce everything to unity. In fact, to understand amounts to succeeding in bringing a multiplicity of data (of
whatever sort) into a unity. It is the famous *reductio ad unum*.
Then and only then we do not proceed further and our mind
rests. In other words, the problem of pluralism appears only to
the intellect. The senses present no difficulty whatsoever in per-
ceiving the irreducible colors. Only when we want to understand
them do we need to know what is color, and not just see the
green alongside the violet. We can accept many colors without
any major obstacle. But can we accept many religions with di-
vergent and incompatible truth claims? The obstacle is in our
thinking. But we cannot and should not renounce thinking.

We should not renounce thinking indeed, but we should neither cripple thinking by reducing it to mere calculus. Truth is
more than mathematical exactness. Truth is an awareness of reality and as such it includes also beauty — necessary distinctions
(but not separations) notwithstanding. Bonaventure, echoing Augustine, defines beauty as a rhythmical or melodious equilibrium
("pulchritudo nihil aliud est quam aequalitas numerosa"), adding
that in beauty this metrical evenness or equality acquires its

proper unity ("ibi autem sunt rationes numerosae ad unum reductae," *Hexaemeron,* VI, 7). Even mathematicians acknowledge that "one" is not a number, and philosophers know that thinking discovers beauty as much as truth and goodness.

My personal identity is not the intelligible unity of the plural elements or factors constitutive of my being, but rather the awareness of the belonging together of those elements or factors.

The second commentary refers to the different use of the principles of identity and noncontradiction in different cultures. I will use the example of the semitic and the indic minds.

The semitic mind thinks of identity by exclusion, that is, by applying in the first place the principle of noncontradiction. A religion is such when it differentiates itself from another one: "you are a christian," amounts therefore to "you are not a hindu" — which takes for granted, of course, that a hindu is a non-christian. The christian identity affirms itself over against the background of not being a hindu. The best a Muslim can say about God, blessed be he, is that he is not like human beings. A believing jew may respect, but will not participate in, hindu idol worship. He is a jew, not a *goy.*

The indic mind, on the contrary, thinks identity in terms of inclusion; it applies in the first place the principle of identity. A religion is such when it identifies itself with the concept of religion. I am a hindu when I am a hindu, and I am all the more a hindu the more I am identified with hinduism as religion, as pure religion — accepting for the sake of argument that hinduism is religion and even a religion. As a hindu I will not feel any scruple in receiving the christian sacraments, although I know they belong to another religion. I will not suspect that I am betraying my hinduism when I indulge in what is most horrendous for the occidental christian mind: the so-called *communicatio in sacris,* participation in the rituals of another religion. When the pope went to India, thousands of hindus went devotedly to receive Holy Communion. A hindu will feel, in a certain way, that when she is a better hindu she will also be a better christian. The best a *vedāntin* will say about Brahman is that It is so totally identical to Itself that there is no place to differentiate It from anything — and certainly not from me. The only authentically true statement of the I, of the true I, is *aham brahman*. To be a hindu and at the same time a non-hindu would be a contradiction; but not to be a christian. Different ways of thinking!

In both cases, however, if I believe in a set of tenets, I cannot believe in the same way and at the same time in a contradictory set of beliefs. But my religious identity is not to be confused with the set of beliefs I adhere to. Faith is not identical to belief, nor religion to a set of doctrines. A nineteenth-century protestant did not share the same beliefs as a catholic. Yet they were both christians and even mutually accused themselves of being heretics.

These reflections lead us to affirm that our identity is inseparable from the way we think our identity, although we may make the distinction between our identity and our interpretation of it. We need to underscore this point lest we forget our own modern individualistic myth. The personal identity of many people is by far not synonymous with the awareness of one's gross body. "Cujus regio eius religio," the famous phrase sounding so ignominious to modern ears, could furnish us with an important historical example. My identity, what I am, does not need to be just the physical body that my senses and my memory witness as being mine. My identity as a jew or as a pole, a calvinist or a hindu cannot be put under one single criterion.

If my mother happens to be from a traditional jewish community, even if she never put a foot in the synagogue, and I acknowledge my jewish origins, I am a jew. If my father belongs to a hindu family, even if he does not believe in any specific tenets, and I do not disown my karma, I am a hindu. If my parents were so-called unbelievers, but had me baptized and I do not disown that rite, I am a christian. If I have taken refuge in the Buddha, the Dharma, and the Sangha, I may be considered a buddhist. If I, in spite of my origins, sincerely worship Allah and recognize Muhammad as his Prophet with the Qur'ān as the revelation of God, I am a Muslim. If I belong to the ibos and have not converted to another religion, generally christianity or islam (and even then I would not be so sure), I am an ibo. And this would apply to most so-called tribal religions. I am saying this to make clear that we cannot apply one single criterion in order to determine the religious identity of a person. If you are a Muslim or a christian, you are a Muslim or a christian forever, in the same way that sometime ago you could not lose your french nationality, even if you took on another citizenship or renounced the french.

How often have we not heard the reproach, generally from outsiders who profess to know better: "But then you are not a christian," or "as a Muslim you cannot say this!" Who has the right to excommunicate the other?

I am ready to defend the thesis that if someone sincerely confesses to be a vaishnava, a catholic, a baha'i, or whatever, and as such is recognized by a community of the same confession, that person is what she affirms herself to be, although she may be considered a heretic by some other groups. Living religions are constantly in a *fluxus quo*. And we all know that often the despised heretics of yesterday are the recognized prophets of tomorrow.

Religious Belonging

Finally we come to grips with the concrete problem of whether we can appertain simultaneously to several religious traditions. It is here that the different traits of what we have been trying to say should come together. In order to be brief I may recur reluctantly to an autobiographical example.

One of the most often quoted and misquoted sentences of mine dates from 1970. It sums up in a certain way over half a century of personal experience. After having spent at that time one-third of my life in India and the rest in the West, I wrote, "I 'left' as a christian, I 'found' myself as a hindu, and I return back as a buddhist, without having ceased to be a christian."

It has been interpreted as if I were saying that I lost my christian identity and instead got a threefold identity. My original paper should prove that I did not mean an eclectic mix of three religions or a doctrinal synthesis of a new religion. I have been insisting that we cannot have a pluralistic system, follow a multiplicity of philosophies, or belong to a plurality of religions. What we have is a personal religiousness which may have integrated, more or less harmoniously, the tenets of several religious traditions. This positive symbiosis does not make us a split personality. We all have a father and a mother, that is, different factors which shape our being. Orthodox christology does not affirm that Christ is half God and half Man, but fully divine and fully human in a personal union.

Leaving aside biology and theology, a metaphor from the neglected area of the geography of religions may be useful here. When the Yamunā and the Ganges meet, the Missouri and the Mississippi, or the Paraná and the Salado, why should we call the continuation of the rivers with a single name giving preference to the Ganges, the Mississippi, and the Paraná? Have the other rivers disappeared? Or is it only a question of power? The waters are indistinguishable and the identity is a new one. Is the Ganges after Allahabad less holy because her waters have been "polluted" by the Yamunā?

Indeed, when the little Assī (now practically disappearing) joins the majestic Mā Gangā, the Assī is proud to have been received by the great river and enjoys the privilege of being also holy. After Varanasi the Assī has become the Gangā, and the Gangā is also happy not to excommunicate the Assī and carry her waters until the very shores of the wide ocean. Here comes again the question of labels. Just for competition regarding length we call one river Missouri/Mississippi. The Yamunā, and much more the invisible Saraswatī are proud to be called Ganges, although who knows if one day the same river meandering through Patna, the buddhist country, will be called the river of the bodhisattvas.

Each river, like each personal religion, is fed by small rivulets of our personal biographies. In recent times, by and large, except for particular cases, the tributaries to our major religions have been small though many. But we should not forget the geography of the past. When the waters of the germanic peoples joined the Latin Tiber, which had already received greek and hebrew water molecules, they became a new river, which we still call christianity in spite of the many hydraulic changes. Should we build, in our technocratic era, gigantic dams to prevent, or worse, to direct according to our strategies, the fresh waters of the life-spending rivers of the world? A dam is eclecticism because the waters are not allowed to flow and are sluiced into an artificial agglomeration.

But there is still more. When meandering through a christian territory I feel a christian, but some who know other lands tend to call me a hindu or a buddhist. And vice versa: when my life flows in a hindu milieu some call me a "pukka" hindu and others a "dangerous" christian. To continue with our rivers and with our remark on labels: the same river flowing in one country is called the "Son of Brahma," the Brahmaputra, and when it bestows its benefits in another land it is called the "Yellow River," the Yaluzangbujiang. Have the tibetans now lost their river? Is it all a question of power? What is the identity of the river?

I am singing basically a single melody in three tones. The first belongs to the heart, the second to the mind, and the third to the spirit.

a. *First: The heart.* We are often shy and tend to demean the matters of the heart. I am saying that I did establish real, affectionate, and active fellowship with those three traditions, to which I have to add the secular community of my fellow citizens in the wide world struggling for justice and searching for truth, irrespective of "confessional" creeds. They are also my people. Anything which touches those communities strikes chords in me which do not weaken those of our common human heritage, and yet they are more particularly sensitive. Indeed, I feel also ashamed or exhilarated when my brothers and sisters at large have committed crimes or performed heroic acts. I feel ashamed of nazism and the slave trade, but I will respect a deeper feeling than mine in a German and in a black american or an african. I am proud of Shakespeare and Ibsen, but Dante and John of the Cross come much closer to my heart. I admire the Qur'ān, but the Vedas speak to me more than the hebrew Bible and the Gospels more than the Analects, although I have more intellectual admiration for Lao Tzu than for Saint James. Each of us is at home somewhere, and this home does not need to be the four walls of a chalet; yet it needs to be a home, a congenial environment of our own. "Yo soy yo y mi circunstancia" was the famous phrase of José Ortega y Gasset. My religious identity is part of my human identity.

Religious identity is neither an automatic fact of birth like that of being a member of a tribe, race, or nation, nor an ideological membership like that of a club, political party, or association. While we don't choose our parents or tribe, and we do choose our club or party, we are somewhat chosen by the religion we accept to belong to. Acceptance, and free acceptance, is here paramount. I call it the feminine element. My religious identity comes as a sort of gift, a kind of grace which comes to me and that I am free to accept, reject, or modify. But I have not two loves when I love my father and my mother or bathe in my hindu and my christian waters. "Le coeur à ses raisons, . . . " (the heart has its reasons that reason does not know [Pascal]) "karmagatir vicitrā . . . " (the course of karma is mysterious and difficult to discern [Yoga Sūtra Bhāṣya II, 13]).

b. *The mind.* To profess one religion or to confess one's religious fellowship is not synonymous with just falling in sympathy with a certain group of people. It is a much more serious matter. It is also an affair of the mind, a question of intellectual honesty. It is an issue of belief, of an enlightened belief. I could not belong to a tradition which tells me to hate my enemy or that there is nothing more than what meets the eye.

This means that the doctrines of a particular religion will have to appear believable to me. And if I have to do with more than one religious tradition I will have to find a personal way of reconciling apparently irreconcilable doctrines. And here the pluralistic attitude is central.

A threefold task needs to be performed here.

1. The discovery of a *fundamental harmony.* We should dig down to the core of those traditions and find whether there are direct contradictions in their fundamental insights. *Satya, karuṇā, agapê,* and *justice* seem to me fundamental insights of those four traditions, all of which open up ways of overcoming selfishness and reaching "transcendence."

2. The search for *human polarities.* We should examine whether many apparently lethal tensions may be nothing but disguised or deformed divergences which, well interpreted or reinterpreted, may be converted into enriching polarities or alternate modes of explaining perennial questions of the human mind.

Between a upanishadic spirituality of interiority and a Christian service to one's neighbor there may be a very fruitful polarity and not an irreconcilable tension. If the belief in reincarnation does not degrade the dignity of the human person by converting her into a mere stepping-stone in a cosmic cycle, I do not see any difficulty in adopting the cosmological hypothesis behind the so-called reincarnation in fair competition with the cosmology underlying heaven and purgatory from a common christian viewpoint.

3. Coping with *irreconcilable doctrines*. We should keep irreconcilable teachings, without distorting them, as expressions of mutually incommensurable formulations of what I may call succinctly the Mystery. No doctrine gives an exhaustive explanation of any religious tenet. A hindu *ātmavāda* and a buddhist *anātmavāda* are irreconcilable, and also incompatible are the metaphysical options of a thomistic and a scotistic christian scholasticism. I may find either a via media, or a plausible reinterpretation, or I should simply let them subsist as valid options, provided I succeed in avoiding strict contradiction. The basic requisite for this third task is obviously to relativize the mutually incommensurable tenets without playing them down or diluting their contents and exigencies. This is not possible if strict rationalism is accepted as the ultimate metron of all reality. But it is not against reason to accept incompatibility, and to live with it, provided we do not allow the *diction* of the contradiction to percolate into the ontic level. The condition is that we recognize the distinction between the ontic and the ontological levels and that we do not absolutize the latter. In other words, there is a transcendence which transcends the two opposite irreconcilable statements. This allows for situating onto different planes the doctrinally contradictory sentences.

The coexistence between particle and wave theories in modern physics may give us a pale example of how to cope with such a situation. The example is pale because in our case we are concerned with something much more problematic than the obedience to our mathematical postulates and to the phenomena which appear to our measuring instruments. Between a theistic and an atheistic system, between *ātmavāda* and *anātmavāda*, there is incompatibility for our understanding (*quoad nos*), but we do not have here a referent like a mathematical postulate or an empirical observation (as in physics). We have instead an unreachable transcendence which we cannot say is exhaustively represented by any of the contradictory statements. We recognize instead the limits of our intellectual faculties. The circumference and the radius are mutually incommensurable, and yet they coexist and are mutually dependent. But there is more.

c. *The spirit.* It is also a matter of the spirit and of the "spirit of the times." It belongs to the *kairos* of our contemporary culture to go a step beyond the religious apartheids of times past — justified as they might have been in a situation which was different from ours. I spoke earlier of mutation. Our religious identity is not reduced to belonging to institutions of the past.

Many a religious constituency is obsolete today. There are religious nationalisms and religious patriotisms which work against the central issue of all religions, which consists precisely in breaking all those bondages which prevent the fulfillment of every being in general and human beings in particular.

A pathetic example of the inadequacy of religious institutions to provide religious identity could be the life and doubts of Simone Weil, who died of physical exhaustion in 1943. She, the jewish "unbeliever," was roman catholic at heart, but her mind did not allow her to follow her heart. Her spirit was more catholic than that of many a roman catholic theologian, but the spirit of the times was not ripe for harvesting such a splendid flower in any confessional field. By remaining in the no-man's-land of religious institutions, she broke through the walls of religious exclusivisms.

Now, in order to bring about the required transformation we have to process step-by-step, and from the very heart of each tradition.

Let me be personal again. I understand and can also speak more than one language as my own. That is, I think from within the universe of each language without translating from another one. This applies of course to religions as languages. Using a christian language I will so wholeheartedly confess that Christ is the truth that I will reverse the sentence, like Gandhi did with

God, and affirm that the truth is Christ. In both cases *truth* stands for ultimate truth, of course — and has little to do with exactness, precision, or accuracy. This Christ, identified with truth, is obviously not a sort of hidden Jesus lurking underneath hinduism or elsewhere in order to "get hindus over," but simply truth.

Nobody has the monopoly on truth, nor do christians have the monopoly on Christ. Christ is simply (at this level of discourse) the christian symbol for truth, but it is neither the only label nor does the word *Christ* reveal all the many other possible aspects of truth. Yet, christians cannot but use this name while confirming that they do not know the breath, length, height, and depth of that mystery which surpasses all knowledge (Eph. 3:18–19).

This is christian language, but I can speak other languages which convey liberating power and saving grace — not only for their respective believers (which is obvious) but for me as well. I am not translating from christianity, but speaking other languages, and I discover not that I am saying "the same" but that it is my selfsame same who sincerely expresses his convictions. It is a parallel language and I understand both.

Reflecting on this fact I submit religions to profound reinterpretations for which I am solely, but conscientiously, responsible. I am a christian whom Christ has led to sit at the feet of the great masters of hinduism and buddhism and become also their disciple. It is my being a hindu-buddhist christian.

This allows me to declare myself a bona fide christian and also a hindu, a buddhist, and a scholar. How I have done this is a life's commitment, and not always an immediately successful one. Yet, hope is also a religious virtue.

But this is not all. From the other end of the spectrum I perform similar steps. I am a hindu whose karma has led him to encounter Christ and a buddhist whose personal effort has led him to similar results regarding the two other traditions.

I could start here from my experience of the *sanātana dharma* which allows me to discover this insight also within christianity and buddhism. Also, Shiva is a living symbol for me. I know by experience that the lingam of Aruṇāchala is more than a stone or a mountain, that the *trika* is more than a dialectical device. But this very insight leads me to search for homeomorphic equivalents within christianity and reinterpret these latter with hindu categories. In short, I discover myself a christian-buddhist-hindu. And I do something similar with buddhism.

What, then, is my religion? Do I not belong simultaneously to the three? Or are they not rather harmoniously transformed in me? Are not all the waters of the Bhagirathī, Alaknandā, Gomatī, Yamunā, Ghāghrā, Son, Assī, Varunā, all waters of the Ganges, once they reach a certain point? I could have said Negro, Japurá, Juruá, Purus, Madeira, and Tapajós, all waters of the Amazon. At a certain moment in life the river is only one, be it carrying waters from Wisconsin, Illinois, Des Moines, Missouri, Arkansas, Minnesota, or Mississippi.

Which label shall we put to our own religiousness? Hindu-catholic? Christian-hindu? Secular-buddhist? Buddhist-hindu? Can we put such labels to the life-giving waters of the rivers? The living waters of our personal religion may carry streams from many sources.

•

What does it all mean? It means a triple fact: a historical newness, a metaphysical challenge, and a religious mutation.

The historical newness is patent. Religions were once upon a time identified with the tribe one belonged to. Their identity afterward was centered in a doctrinal creed that was supposed to be the uniting force of religious institutions. Broadly speaking, this is what today we call religions. The coming historical period will put the emphasis on the experiential factor. Religions will be primarily identified by the set of faith experiences which will slowly find their appropriate doctrines and found their more adequate structures and institutions. Tradition is not sheer repetition of the past but a "handing over" (*traditio*) of the accumulated experiences conveniently transformed. The polymorphic characters of hinduism may give us an inkling of what I am saying.

The metaphysical challenge could be said to be another name for pluralism. The awareness of external, sociological, organizational, and other differences among religions leads us to renounce any type of exclusivism. The religious dimension of human beings, or religiousness, is more than a mere sociological construct. Religions have a mystical core.

The metaphysical challenge deabsolutizes all our ways of thinking and even of being. Religions do not need to follow already known and trodden ways. Reality, and authentic religiousness as well, as human parts of realization (salvation, liberation . . .), are radical novelties and not mere conclusions of the past. Our parliament is not a museum. It should be a crucible.

Religions are not immovable and artificial dams to contain water in order to produce power. Religions are flowing rivers nurtured by high glaciers of rishis and prophets, distinct sources from thinkers and past traditions enlivened by nearby clouds from contemporary history — all coming from the heavens in order to bring life to the earth and to human beings.

The religious mutation is not the fruit of any violent revolution or attack from the outside, but the fruit of a growth from within each tradition so that the way is not through apostasy or abandonment, but through a higher fidelity to the unfathomable grace of the Spirit, which, as the jewish Bible says, is "a silent Wind" (1 Kings 19:12).

We are not only cocreators of our own lives. We are also cocreators of our religions. The future of humanity depends on this. The coming millennium will be a "new Name" brought about by a radical human *metanoia* or it will not be. The earth can wait. She will still be there. The human race cannot. Either a transformation takes place or we disappear from the face of the earth. As the Kathopanishad says:

> *asti-na-asti:*
> To exist or not to exist.
> This is the question. And our responsibility.

Chapter 3

"Our Religions" in a Religiously Plural World

Harvey Cox, Arvind Sharma, Seyyed Hossein Nasr, and Masao Abe

"Our Religions" as the title of this chapter refers both to our own religions and to a book which bears that title and was released at a Parliament of World's Religions at Chicago by HarperSanFrancisco as its contribution to the centennial celebration of the 1893 World's Parliament of Religions. The fact that each chapter in this book was written by a scholar who himself belonged to the tradition he was writing about constituted the unique feature of the book.

In order to commemorate the release of the book, a panel was organized by the Conference on Pluralism, in which four contributors were asked to reflect on the impact religious plurality has had on their understanding or presentation of their own religious tradition in the modern world. They responded as follows.

Harvey Cox (Christianity)

How is my understanding of my own faith tradition and my presentation of that tradition affected by the fact that it takes place in a religiously plural world? Somehow an old gospel song comes to mind, a song that many of you have probably heard: *Will the Circle Be Unbroken?* In a phrase that song catches something very deep in the Jewish and Christian traditions: a vision of an ultimately united human family across the ages, across the continents, across the faiths. Will the circle be unbroken? As I think about interfaith dialogue in which I have participated in recent years, I think about the way in which the circle has been expanded and strengthened, but also about chinks which remain in that circle, and about ways in which the circle has inadvertently been impaired by the emergence of interfaith dialogue. I would like to comment on this. The emergence of interfaith dialogue is a gift to each other. Listening to and speaking with people from religious traditions, not just scholars of those traditions but practitioners of those traditions, is to my mind a gift of God and one for which I am thankful. However, one also thinks about the absences and I want to mention two absences today that trouble me in the presentation of that vision of the unbroken circle. Both of these absences are visible today.

The first is the absence of those people whose response to any kind of religious claim is similar to the advice often given to young people about drugs: They "just say no." These are the people who are puzzled, angered, bored, put off by any or all religious claims. I am not speaking today about Madalyn Murray O'Hare or other militant atheists. I'm speaking about my brother-in-law, about your brother-in-law perhaps, about the people who seem to live their lives without any need for or interest in any of the claims in any religious tradition and yet seem to be serene, compassionate, and courageous people — the gentle skeptics. I am not talking about smart-alecky college professors. I am talking about the people for whom all our sermons and darshans fall on deaf ears and glazed eyes. Yet these are also our fellow human beings. They are the people, incidentally, for whom Dietrich Bonhoeffer, my favorite theologian, developed a special affection when he was in prison. They were the people who seemed to be able to struggle against the Nazis unto death without the consolation of any kind of religious faith. He was impressed with these people, and he promised that once he was released from prison he would try to develop what he called a "nonreligious interpretation of the Gospel." He never got a chance to do that because he was executed by the Nazis in 1945.

From my point of view faith is not an accomplishment. It is a gift and therefore one cannot think any less of those human beings among us who do not seem to exhibit this gift. It would be too bad to create a new circle of religiously sensitive, advanced, and dialogical people which closes out this very large segment of our fellow human beings who do not have the gift of faith, the nonbelievers. Can pluralism include them as well?

There is a second and even more troublesome absence that I'd like to talk about and that is the absence here, as it was also evident in 1893 at the former Parliament of Religions, of those whose attitude toward interfaith dialogue is also "Thank you, but no." I think that dialogue is a blessing, but I have to remind all of us that it has exacted its price because in each of the traditions represented here what has emerged is a dialogical wing — in Christianity, Hinduism, Buddhism, and Islam — and a strongly antidialogical wing, a party which is opposed to everything that we are about here. Most of you know something about this party, the antidialogical party. This absence of the fellow believers in our own traditions who say no to dialogue, troubles me because I think it can, on the part of those of us who are committed to dialogue, produce a new kind of self-congratulatory elitism.

In my conversations with such people I have discovered they are not all bigots or fundamentalists or fanatics. They have a variety of reasons why they choose not to be part of this kind of conversation. For some it is simply a misguided innocence that we are involved in here; for others, it is religiously suspect. For still others it is simply a waste of valuable energy and time. Better we should be at prayer or engaged in acts of mercy and justice. These are not all bigots. In fact, just after the 1893 World Religions Conference, a French Roman Catholic priest tried to organize a similar meeting in Paris and invited Count Leo Tolstoy, perhaps the most admired Christian of that period. Tolstoy politely declined the invitation. He said he did not believe that such conversations and conferences contributed to drawing us closer either to God or to each other.

Now my question to my fellow panelists and to you is: how do we then view our serious co-religionist who "just say no" to what we are doing here? I have to admit that the strong temptation on my part is to ignore them or avoid them. It is far more rewarding to have conversations with my good friend Arvind Sharma or with my old friend Masao Abe, who first introduced me to the temples of Nara, than to have sharp-edged and sometimes unpleasant conversations with fellow Christians who think I am giving the farm away because I'm engaged in interfaith dialogue. But I have to come to believe that it is just as important, at least for me, to cultivate the *intra*faith dialogue as well as the *inter*faith dialogue. Otherwise we could be heading for a new alliance, a new circle of the dialogical wings of each of our religious traditions, separated by a deepening chasm from the antidialogical wings. We would have a circle, but it would still be broken — only broken in a new way.

Consequently in recent years I have tried to spend as much time in this internal intrafaith conversation, sometimes frustrating, sometimes difficult, as I do in what might be called the external or the interfaith dialogue. I have discovered two things which I would like to close my contribution here with. The first is the common assumption that people opposed to interfaith dialogue will not converse about their reasons and will not enter into any conversations at all on this subject. This is simply wrong. In the past few years I have probably logged as many hours at Evangelical and Pentecostal churches and conferences and schools as I have in interfaith events such as this. And I have learned that such conversations *are* possible and — at least from the point of view of my tradition — enormously important. We would gain nothing by great advances in interfaith dialogue at the price of terrible divisions within our own traditions, including my own. But I have also learned that these conversations are possible only if I keep a second principle in mind. It is that in this internal intrafaith dialogue, I need to grant my dialogue partner the same benefit of the doubt, the same attempt to understand his or her perspective, to get inside his or her point of view, as I have tried to learn to exercise in my conversations with Hindus and Buddhists and Muslims; sometimes succeeding and sometimes failing. That is, I cannot assume at the outset that the spiritual reasoning or the intellectual assumptions which guide their decision not to participate in interfaith dialogue are any less serious than mine or ours. So I cannot enter into that conversation any more than I can enter conversations with Muslims or Hindus in an attempt to proselytize or convert or persuade. I can enter it in good faith, listening, trying to understand the other perspective, trusting that the spirit will lead that conversation in whatever direction it should go. Some of these conversations have been enormously profitable and helpful. I am thankful for them, too, because in one sense that is a gift of grace against even more difficulties than the ones represented by the conversation at this table. Too often, however, when I become frustrated with this internal conversation, I find myself slipping into a frame of mind which I really do not like to see in myself. That is a kind of dismissive or condescending attitude toward those whose rejection of interfaith dialogue I regret and deplore. I begin to think of them as representing the dark and selfish and narrow and less informed and ignorant perspective, while I of course represent the enlightened, advanced, intelligent, compassionate: you can add to the list. Then it dawns on me, however, that this is precisely the set of attitudes I have tried not to deploy in conversations with people in other religious traditions. Why should they be deployed against those in my own tradition, also the children of God? What does thinking in such a negative manner about them contribute in the long run?

Occasionally at this and other interfaith conferences, I confess that I have heard this negative sentiment now and then, and I want to blow a rather sharp whistle about it. That is, I have heard it voiced that we here somehow represent the enlightened wings of our various traditions, the more evolved sectors, the more thoughtful, intelligent — maybe even the more "spiritual" — parts of our traditions. It is sometimes said, and often really implied, that those who are not here represent all the opposites. But it is dangerous to create yet another "other" to be on the outside of the new circle we are creating here. This simply produces a kind of a elitism, a religious elitism and a further broken circle.

So to my fellow panelists: I have enjoyed working with you enormously on this wonderful book. To all of them and to all of you, let me say that I rejoice more than I can possibly say in your presence here as a gift which the spirit has given to us: it is a precious gift. Let us be aware, however, that our enlarged circle is still broken and that there are absences. There are those who are not here, and let us strive somehow not to displace them or exclude them from our vision of the circle that someday, in God's good time, will be unbroken, and we may all be very surprised when we look around, at who is here.

Arvind Sharma (Hinduism)

I think my reflection belongs to a slightly different and more personal domain but one which, I think, will branch out into a more public one as I proceed. The moment of truth or, rather, I should say, a moment of truth overtook me regarding the book while I was conversing with Professor Liu, who has contributed the chapter on Taoism to the book, while we were having dinner in Cambridge one evening. He leaned over toward me and asked, "Tell me, Professor Sharma, do you believe in all you are going to write about Hinduism?" A long pause ensued. It was followed by a longer pause. I was still verbally floundering when he spoke again: "I do not want to put you in a spot. You do not have to answer it if you don't want to." "Oh, no," I explained. "On the contrary, I would very much like to answer the question. I am just wondering how to do so without doing injustice to my position by either exaggerating or understating it." The conceptual, verbal struggle for precision finally yielded an outcome. I said to Professor Liu: "I do not disbelieve in it." Professor Liu broke out in a laugh. Somehow, I got the feeling that he knew the space I was in, to use a New Age expression. The question he asked was one which, subsequently, I often asked myself and which induced further investigation and, perhaps, even introspection. And these crystallized in the form of two comments which I made to myself. Now, one of them was: "If one lives in a haunted house, does it mean that one believes in ghosts?" And the second reflection was: "To say that I don't believe in something does not mean that I deny its possibility. It only means that I do not have significant evidentiary material to make it publicly verifiable." I now realize that what I was trying to do then was to distinguish between an "insider" and a "believer."

I can unequivocally say that I wrote the chapter on Hinduism as an insider. I would be compelled to be equivocal if I were asked whether I wrote it as a believer. And I think I would panic if I were asked if I wrote it as a true believer. This equivocation derives, I think, in part, from the fact that I was writing about Hinduism in a religiously plural world. And it is compounded by the attitude of Hinduism itself toward religious plurality, which it encourages. My reluctance to commit myself more completely to the specific Hindu set of beliefs and practices was not the result of skepticism about them. It seemed to result from a recognition of pluralism, out of the fear that if I placed myself too close to a specificity, I might be positioning myself too far from the other traditions of the world — a situation which made me feel uncomfortable as a Hindu, lest an excess of commitment to Hinduism might bar my access to traditions not so called.

The fact that I was writing about my tradition in a religiously plural world involved me and perhaps involved others as well — and I now move on to a second point — in a tension between the ethnic and the universal. I would like to clarify this. I am using the word *ethnic* here not in the sense of Shinto, Judaism, and Hinduism being ethnic religions in the sense that one's membership in these traditions is predicated on being born in them. A little reflection discloses the fact that most Christians and Muslims and Buddhists are also, after all, born into their religions — notwithstanding the fact that their ancestors may have converted to those religions long ago or even recently. And, to the extent that this is true, I wonder whether they, too, do not experience this tension between the ethnic (as now defined) and the universal in relation to their own traditions. So this is another way in which the fact that I was writing about Hinduism in a religiously plural world affected my presentation of it: by causing this tension to surface.

Yet another way in which the context of religious plurality affected my presentation was the relative space devoted to the discussion of certain issues. This point is best made by asking the hypothetical question: How would my discussion of Hinduism be different if I were writing this chapter, not for the general reader, but for my fellow Hindus? For one thing, I would have devoted more space to a discussion of the caste system. It looms large in the outside world's perception of Hinduism and is so widely associated with it that I started with the working assumption of this aspect of Hinduism being common knowledge, and so addressed its stereotype rather than the institution itself. I might have done the same about the stereotypes regarding attitudes to social service and women in Hinduism. But here, I was assisted by the presence of figures like Mahatma Gandhi and Mrs. Indira Gandhi, who constituted living repudiations of at least the cruder fallacies in this regard. But to revert to the question of the caste system, how, precisely, was my presentation affected by the fact that the chapter was intended for a religiously plural audience? In the context of this audience, I suggest that while the reader may be inclined to regard the caste system as essential to Hinduism, the modern Hindu tends to regard it as only specific to it: a special form of social stratification specific to it as other forms are, or may be, to other religions or societies. If I was writing this chapter for my fellow Hindus, I would have made another point, and which I would like to make now. The Hindu sacred texts allow for marriage between members of the four *varṇas* all over the country; but typically these marriages took place within much smaller circles. This is what J. Duncan M. Derrett means, I think, when he asserts that in the matter of marriage, the Hindus in the past were even more conservative than their scriptures!

A fourth and final way in which my presentation of Hinduism was affected by a religiously plural context may be identified in the following way. While drafting a chapter on Hinduism, one can keep the country (that is, India) primarily in mind, or, by contrast, the world in general. This statement must, of course, be understood in a relative sense, as neither dimension can be excluded. It is a question of adjusting the rival claims, to the extent that they are rival claims. My own approach in the chapter could be encapsulated aphoristically as — and I plagiarize unashamedly — write locally, think globally.

Now, what does thinking globally mean? One meaning which could be attached to the expression is to think in terms of global trends. What, then, are the global trends in the field of religion? It seems that pluralism, secularism, and fundamentalism would, perhaps, qualify as global trends. And each, by itself, provides a plot for the story of religion as it is told to contemporary readers. It is when they are treated together, however, in a constellation, as it were — pluralism, secularism, and fundamentalism — that the plot really thickens, especially in the case of India. For pluralism, by itself, does not present an entirely novel situation in the Indian context. Pluralism in modern times may contain novel elements, but the situation of religious pluralism, as such, is not a novelty for India. What is novel in Indian history is the employment of the concept of secularism to deal with this pluralism. (And here, I mean secularism in the accepted Western sense.) In order to understand the implications of this, one needs to rehearse certain historical facts and formulate certain conceptual distinctions.

To begin with, American secularism was and is a response to religious pluralism. However, American secularism was originally a response, not to a plurality of religions, but to the plurality of Christian sects. Now, of course, I am open here to correction by Professor Cox. I know the presence of Judaism complicates this point a bit. But essentially, American secularism was a response to Christian sectarianism, or rather to the plurality as represented by Christian sects, and not to the plurality represented by the presence of different religions. It was a political device to handle intrareligious pluralism rather than interreligious pluralism — a point already made by Professor Cox: that of the distinction between the two. In India, secularism was introduced to handle not intrareligious pluralism but interreligious pluralism — that is, within Hinduism. Pluralism within Hinduism is handled by the Indian state directly according to the Indian constitution. The state claims to be secular, essentially, in an interreligious context. It has, however, not hesitated in dealing with intrareligious matters only in the case of Hinduism. This asymmetrical behavior of the Indian state is what has rendered the concept of secularism itself questionable to many Hindus. Two other sets of conceptual distinctions are also important.

One set pertains to the exact nature of the relationship between state and church in a secular state. This relationship can take three forms. It can be neutral as in the case of the United States; it can be negative as in the case of the former communist countries; and it can be positive as in a hypothetical case in which a state chooses to deliberately promote religious harmony.

A second set of distinctions also needs to be drawn: between a secular state, a secular society, and a secular nation. The United Kingdom possesses an established church, so it is not a secular state. But, to all intents and purposes, it is a secular society. The United States is a secular state. But it is a secular society? The answer to this could go either way. It is a secular society in the sense that large areas of life are free of church control. But it is a religious society in the sense that the various religious denominations are vigorously active. Is America a secular nation? The identification of a civil religion in the United States would incline one to answer in the affirmative. But in 1892 and subsequently, I am told, the Supreme Court declared the United States to be a Christian nation. One is tempted to ask whether the way out of the present impasse in India lies in declaring India a secular state but a Hindu nation. While we are on the topic, it is worth noting that this impasse to which the suggestion is offered as a possible solution itself is the outcome of the religiously plural context in which Hinduism is operating in India, and that Hindu fundamentalism is a response to other fundamentalisms.

To conclude, then: to say that we live in a religiously plural world is a cliché; to say that we live in a religiously plural world — especially after having spent four or five days in these discussions — sounds like a cliché. To say that religions are changing all the time is a truism. But to say that, if you change, I change — perhaps this amounts to an insight.

Seyyed Hossein Nasr (Islam)

I wish I could spend the fifteen minutes allotted to me to simply carry out a discussion with Professor Cox about what he said, including faith being simply a gift and therefore those who have not received this gift have no responsibility for it. In fact, acting as God's representatives on earth (to use an Islamic term, a term which is of course open to a great deal of discussion in relation to the question of whether we can take away responsibility from human beings) is the consequence of our possessing a divine norm. By virtue of this norm we can say that — whether or not we have received the gift of faith in addition to the gift of being human — we have the responsibility that the human state implies. The Islamic perspective would assert that we have received the responsibility that goes with faith with the very gift of being human. It is not therefore possible to separate the two. I just wanted to say how significant even small forays are across religious borders. I shall try to limit my comments not to my humble role in the preparation of this wonderful volume, but to concern myself with the larger role that I have had for some thirty-seven years now, since my early twenties when I was at Harvard University trying to carry out religious dialogue and to present Islam to a non-Islamic and essentially Western audience.

The first conference I ever attended on religious dialogue took place in the Atlas Mountains of Morocco. It was arranged by Catholic monks, and among the scholars present was the great French Islamicist and orientalist Louis Massignon, perhaps the greatest academic authority that the West has ever produced in the field of Islamic studies. Talking about the question of religious dialogue (I quote almost verbatim from his French statement, which I have never forgotten), he said, "It is now too late for conferences to solve the problems of the world; the only thing to do now is to perform the prayer of the heart." That, of course, was a correct statement in a deep sense: that inner prayer is the highest form of dialogue. Nevertheless, as the hands of destiny would have it, I have been caught during the last thirty-seven years exactly in the situation of attending conferences on religious dialogue and have been in the process of trying to explain the very idea of the multiplicity of religions from the metaphysical, traditional point of view, as seen from the perspective of the *religio perennis*, especially as expounded by Frithjof Schuon, in addition to trying to explain Islam to an essentially Western audience.

I have been very much aware of the problems in the West mentioned by Professor Cox. But these are problems very different from what one faces in other parts of the world. Ecumenism in the West has oftentimes meant the losing or withering away or diluting of the religious structures of a particular religious community; hence the opposition which many members of various religious communities have expressed (to which Professor Cox alluded). I am here reminded of the saying of a European scholar. A devout Christian friend of mine once said that the best thing to do is to have a new motto: "O all antiecumenical forces of the world, unite." If understood properly, this is one of the solutions to the problem posed by Professor Cox.

But let me turn more specifically to what I feel are the fundamental conditions for the presentation of one's own religious perspective in a pluralistic situation, and then say a few words about the particular case of Islam, which presents certain difficulties for the West at this particular moment of history, difficulties which are unique as far as the West is concerned. The most important condition, I believe, is that whoever is envisaged by us as the audience for our presentation, our first criterion must be to remain faithful to the truth. That is the most important of all factors. That is, one cannot under any condition modify the truth for the sake of expediency. Let us just remember that when Honen and Rumi and Śaṅkarācārya were writing those incredible texts, they did not have the Chicago audience of 1993 in mind. They were addressing a particular audience of their own society with its own language, images, symbols. But because they expressed the truth, we still read their works, whereas today, who reads the books of Renouvier, who was the most famous philosopher in France in the 1890s? How many people in this room have even heard of his name? Probably one or two Christian theologians or specialists of modern Western philosophy but very few other people. We still read the classical masters who lived in much earlier periods because they remained faithful to at least some aspect of the truth. The most important factor in the presentation of one's own religion is that of clinging to the truth. Of course one might say that one does not know all the truth about one's tradition and that at the heart of every tradition the highest truth is only known to God and the great saints. Nevertheless, to the extent that one can participate in the truth of the particular religion to which one belongs, one must always remain faithful to it, whether the world likes it or not. This is a major consideration, and this point is not really such a small point even though it seems so obvious. Much of the dialoguing of the past fifty years has in fact been based on eclipsing the truth to some extent in order to accommodate the situation. And that is really the deepest reason why, in the Western context, some of the most profound representatives of Western religions have been totally uninterested in dialogue. This is true of Orthodox Judaism, true of Greek Orthodoxy, true of traditional Catholicism, and this is certainly true of many of the conservative Protestant schools of thought and of theology in various churches. In the other worlds, the non-Western worlds, where certain people do carry on dialogue, many of them in fact are also at the fringe of the central teachings of their religions and are trying to replace truth by expediency in order to be accommodating while many of the most profoundly religious people show no interest in religious dialogue.

One of the great tragedies for traditional religions in the whole exercise of so-called dialoguing in the last few decades is that this activity was begun by and large (not completely, but mostly) by the already modernized West. It was begun mostly by the less traditional circles of America rather than Europeans, and when it occurred in Europe, it was mainly in northern Europe where the hold of traditional forms of religion was less extensive than in the southern countries. We should note that interest in dialogue has not been so extensive in the Spanish, Portuguese, Greek, Italian, and eastern European worlds as in the northern countries until quite recently. Dialoguing in the same sense that we are now using was mostly a phenomenon of northern Europe and America, because of the advent of modernization and revitalization as well as a set of other complicated reasons into whose details I will not go here. In any case, what has usually occurred is that dialoguers in the West have sought to find partners who are their own "clones," who think just like they do. The result has often been wonderful harmony between the two sides. However, the other persons have often not represented any important point of view or perspective within the world to which they belong. I have been an observer of such a phenomenon for a long, long time. Many from the non-Western and more specifically Islamic world (I should be very frank) have been darlings of those interested in religious dialogue in the West, that is, people who are quoted all the time by Western authors as being Islamic partners in dialogue. But rarely would one of their books on dialogue be read with wide approval in the Islamic world itself. In fact, a few of you present in this audience would be very unhappy if such books were to be translated into Islamic languages. Now this situation does not bring about the possibility of any serious discourse. Therefore, we come back to the centrality of the question of remaining faithful to the truth as traditionally understood. This is far from being a secondary matter. It is at the heart of all serious attempts at religious dialogue.

The second point to consider is that we must remember how our message would be understood by the audience which we are addressing. And here there comes into play that art given by God as a gift to some people, the art known in Islam as understanding the "language of the birds," which God taught to Solomon. Symbolically and esoterically, knowing the language of the birds means the possibility of penetrating the language of other universes of discourse. Usually, we human beings cannot understand the language of the birds. The fact that Solomon could understand it means symbolically that God had given him the power of understanding a religious "language" not his own. Now this gift makes it possible for those who do not possess this art to learn from those who do have it and who are able to present their own tradition in a language which is comprehensible to those to whom they are addressing themselves without distortion and with the purpose of creating mutual understanding. This is a very difficult task for non-Western scholars belonging as most of them do to worlds where tradition is still strong and careful as they have been to respect the accepted categories of thought and belief of those they are addressing. Many Western scholars, however, do not usually believe that they have that problem at all (there being of course certain honorable exceptions). So many Western scholars have tried to present Christianity, let us say, to the Islamic world or the Hindu world, in their capacity as missionaries. In the majority of cases (there are always exceptions) their goal has been to bring about an understanding of Christianity to Islam or to Hinduism or to Buddhism not so much with the purpose of *explaining* but of seeking to *convert* them to their own point of view. They have not been interested in relating the truths of Christianity by creating relationships with the sacred universe of those whom they have been addressing but in destroying that sacred universe.

In contrast, the role of non-Western scholars, people such as Professor Abe, Professor Sharma, and myself (Tu Wei-ming from China would have made four) is one of trying to be respectful of the traditions we are addressing and to look at the situation from the point of view, the inner point of view of those traditions while remaining true to our own tradition. This is a different task. It requires precisely to be able to address a message to a primarily Western audience which one knows well enough, not only linguistically but also in an intellectual and spiritual way, so that the message is both authentic and meaningful. In this context the Islamic world has been very inept in being able to produce a large number of scholars able to make the Islamic message understood in the West in such a way that people would really grasp it in an authentic fashion. The Muslims did a much better job five hundred years ago when they were in India — a much better job. The Islamic world by and large produces many books with this purpose in mind, books which in fact are fine to read for people who are already Muslims, sitting in Cairo or Riyadh, but most Westerners do not understand what such books are even talking about.

We have been unsuccessful in this attempt, but this is nevertheless a very important task that must be carried out. And this task, for present-day scholarship, almost always involves knowing the West well. Very few Muslim scholars carry out dialogue right now with China. All of that could, of course, change in the future. In fact, with Tu Wei-ming we are planning now a major dialogue of Confucianism and Islam in the light of all that is written about the clashes of civilization, to avoid the confrontation of civilization about which some people speak. But that has not as yet taken place. When I write something on Islam I have in mind what my colleagues in American and European universities, or scholars of religion, or people of good heart in the West would understand by it. If I were to write something for China, it would be very different. There are a hundred million Muslims living in China, where Muslims have lived for thirteen hundred years. Certain provinces of China have mosques which date from the second Islamic century. There have been exchanges, cultural and otherwise, between Persia and China for two millennia, and especially during the Islamic period. But that would be a story for another day.

As far as the actual situation is concerned, usually the presentation of non-Western religions (and here I limit myself to Islam) in the present-day context has, almost always, the West in mind. Even Muslim scholars writing in Pakistan and India, who might be addressing Hinduism, are they really addressing Hinduism in itself? Often they are also addressing each other but with the West in mind. This is one of the evident realities of present-day dialogue, which is almost completely Eurocentric or Euro-American-centric. It becomes global only to the extent that the particular culture of the West has spread globally, and there are therefore people in various lands all over the world who understand its language and perspective. To fully comprehend the audience whom one is addressing in religious dialogue is in any case, the second condition to be considered for serious religious dialogue. To fulfill this condition requires an art and also a scholarship which is not easy to come by.

The third important task is to present that truth in such a manner that it will still be comprehensible to the followers of the tradition whose truth one is expressing. And this brings me to a delicate point. If my chapter on Islam were right now to be translated into Persian, Arabic, Turkish, Malay, or Urdu and presented in Islamic countries, what would the readers say? Would they say that the author of this work has been brainwashed by Western ideas, or even worse that he has been bought off? Would they say that he does not know his own tradition and what he is talking about?

In each society you can castigate someone by branding him with certain names. They could just call a person a philosopher or a Sufi in certain Arab countries in order to dismiss him. Or would they say, "Yes, what is written is recognizable to us"? They could say that they wished he would have emphasized a particular point more than another but they should not have to say, "This is not our perspective. This is not Islam, but some other religion." Much of the dialoguing that has gone on during the last few decades by Muslim dialoguers — especially when dealing with very complicated issues such as feminism, theological definitions (e.g., the theological definitions of the Trinity in Christianity), sacred community, as far as Judaism and Islam are concerned, sacred land, and other delicate issues — has usually been carried out by those most satisfactory to their Western partners but least acceptable to the communities which they are supposed to be representing. And this is of course a major obstacle to be overcome if there is to be real understanding across religious frontiers.

Now let me conclude by pointing out that all the points I have made apply to non-Western religions in general, but the case of presenting Islam is especially difficult, displaying certain difficulties not shared by the other traditions. Nearly everybody who studies Taoism in America loves it, whereas many people who study Islam in the West are in one way or another opposed to it and certainly show little love for it. We are dealing with a difficult situation which cannot be avoided easily. Much of this difficulty is the fault of the Islamic world itself, but much of it is also the fault of political and economic motives present in the West. If a member of the Mafia is arrested in New York, the American media will never say that a *Catholic* has just been arrested in New York. Or if somebody with a Jewish background were to carry out a theft on Wall Street, they would never say that a *Jewish* swindler has just robbed such and such a sum of money. Or in the terrible war that goes on in Northern Ireland, no one talks about Protestant or Catholic bombs. I was there a few months ago when a bomb exploded in the city of London. Thank God, nobody ever said the *Catholic* bombers are at it again. One would never think in those terms, but as soon as the Oklahoma City bombing took place, in the very first minute many media said that a *Muslim* was suspected of carrying out that heinous act. All of the other revisions of the news during the next few months did little to erase the impression created by the original announcement.

In such a situation, the presentation of Islam is doubly difficult, but it is not impossible, because no matter how difficult the situation, there are always human beings of understanding, of intelligence, and of good intention who are willing to listen to the truth. And in fact these stringent impediments to mutual understanding which come up are precisely the challenges which scholars dealing with the multiplicity of religions are called upon to confront. I think that with Japan bashing going on and the Japanese becoming more and more Asianized or with the rise of Confucianism in China, it could happen that in the future Islam will have some partners around the Pacific in receiving blows of a nonreligious kind, but couched in the dress of religion.

In any case, whatever happens, I believe that we must remain firmly bound to these three basic criteria of, first, to always remain faithful to the truth for which we are born and for which we must live and die; second, to try always to understand the audience whom we are addressing with love, with compassion, with empathy, and also with discernment; and third, always to have the humility to see things from the authentic point of view of our own religion and not hold a position for the sake of expediency that would be so far-fetched as to distort the truths of our religion because of our own distance from our religious community. People can understand their own position in the depths of their heart. Those who are out on a limb in relation to a particular religious community should not present themselves as if speaking for the community as a whole. That is really dishonest and can only result in further misunderstanding. I believe that this book, thanks to the great efforts of Professor Sharma and others, is one of the first collective works to appear in the English language in which many of these issues are addressed and the conditions mentioned above fulfilled. Therefore I hope that it will be an important step in bringing about a greater genuine understanding among religions.*

Masao Abe (Buddhism)

I have engaged in Buddhist-Christian dialogue for the past thirty years. Here, in this panel, I would like to talk about the impact of such a dialogue on my self-understanding as a Buddhist. There are at least the following three issues to be discussed in this re-

---

*This section is based on an oral presentation made by the author on the occasion.

gard. That is, my understanding of *śūnyatā*, Buddhist ethics, and the Buddhist view of history. Due to the restriction of time, however, I will have to reserve my comments to the first two issues — my understanding of *śūnyatā* and Buddhist ethics. I wrote this because, originally, I was informed that each panelist might be able to speak just ten minutes and not more than ten minutes. But when I came here, I heard that each panelist might speak for fifteen minutes. So, perhaps, I will not omit the third issue — that is, the Buddhist view of history.

I introduced the Buddhist notion of *śūnyatā*, or emptiness as the ultimate reality in Buddhism, at the Buddhist-Christian dialogue. I was always asked how such a negative notion as emptiness could be the ultimate reality without falling into nihilism. How can human personality be comprehended on the basis of an impersonal notion such as emptiness? How can ethics and history be grounded in Buddhism by taking emptiness as its ultimate principle? In the course of trying to answer these questions, I became painfully aware of the fact that the term *emptiness*, although it is the usual English translation for the Sanskrit original, *śūnyatā*, can be quite misleading. In your language, "emptiness" always means something negative. "This box is empty." There is no candy in there. "This room is empty." There is no person...nothing, you know. So that the usual meaning of the English term is "emptiness" or "void." The Buddhist ultimate reality is called *śūnyatā*, which literally means empty, or emptiness. So the Western reaction is naturally to ask how such a negative term can indicate ultimate reality without falling into nihilism.

Fundamentally speaking, the term *śūnyatā* is not a metaphysical notion but a religious and a soteriological one. In reality, *śūnyatā* points to the Buddhist insight that all things are without a self-nature and are nonsubstantial. Hence all things are interdependent and involve mutually interpenetrating relationships. The meaning of the term *śūnyatā* indicates that there is no fixed, substantial reality, unchangeable reality in anything in the universe. For instance, American people often talk about California as the West Coast. Then people often understand the state of California as an entity or substance called the "West Coast." But

California may be called the "East Coast" from the point of view of Hawaii or Japan. And California also can be called the "South Coast" from the point of view of British Columbia, and so forth. So even though we usually call it the West Coast, it has no fixed substance named "West Coast." It is only a relational notion. Nevertheless, we often substantialize, reify the concept around it as if that object is an unchangeable, fixed notion.

When we come to the problem of good and evil, or right and wrong, and so forth, this kind of reification or substantialization creates a very serious problem of human life. Buddhism emphasizes that although there is a substance in each thing, there is no absolute, enduring substance in everything — including the human self and the notion of the divine. Once we realize that there is no such fixed and enduring substance of each thing, each thing can be interpenetrating, interdependent, and relational. And that is the meaning of śūnyatā. When one awakens to śūnyatā, nonsubstantiality in all things, one is emancipated from substantialization of, and attachment to, them. And one realizes the interdependent relationality of all things in the world — including oneself. Thus I came to realize that although the term śūnyatā is a noun and may suggest a static state of emptiness, it should be understood as a verb to indicate emptying or nonsubstantializing. In fact, the real meaning of śūnyatā is a pure function of emptying, including the emptying of śūnyatā itself. For if śūnyatā is fixed and substantialized, it is no longer true śūnyatā. True śūnyatā is a complete emptying, self-negating function — not a state — without any existence. Thus through dialogue with Christian colleagues, I came to understand dynamic śūnyatā (that is, the dynamic nature of śūnyatā) and tried to make the positive and soteriological meanings of śūnyatā more explicit.

Reflecting on this change in my thinking, recently, I have been emphasizing that śūnyatā represents a boundless openness — it is not a mere void — free from any sort of centrism, including egocentrism, anthropocentrism, and even theocentrism. It is completely free from any kind of centrism because it is boundlessly open to all directions. There is no fixation at all. Therefore, in śūnyatā, all things, without exception, are realized as it is in pristine suchness, and yet, as interrelated and mutually interpenetrating. So in this boundless openness, everything is realized just as it is. Bamboo is bamboo. A pine tree is a pine tree. An oak tree is an oak tree, you know. A dog is a dog. A cat is a cat. I am I, and you are you. And everything or everyone is realized just as it is because there is no single principle into which everyone must be reduced.

Through the dialogue with Christian colleagues, I also came to realize that the Christian notion of *kenosis* is very important not only within Christianity but also in Buddhist-Christian dialogue. The Epistle to the Philippians states: "The Son of God emptied himself, taking the form of a servant... becoming obedient even unto death, yes death on the cross" (see Phil. 2:7–8). This *kenosis*, that is, self-emptying of the Son of God, will express the love of God. According to the traditional interpretation, however, the Son of God became a human without God ceasing to be God. That is a traditional understanding of the self-emptying of the Son of God. Although the Son of God emptied himself, God the Father never emptied himself. That is a traditional understanding. But, in my view of God, God is really all! Hence God the Father must have emptied himself even while the Son of God emptied himself. Without the self-emptying of God the Father, the self-emptying of the Son of God is inconceivable. The *kenosis* of Christ must have its origin in the *kenosis* of God. Thus, at the East-West religions encounter conference in Honolulu, Hawaii, in 1983, I delivered a paper called "The Kenotical God and the Dynamic *Śūnyatā*." To me, the notion of the kenotical God is extremely important for our Buddhist-Christian dialogue. When we clearly realize the notion of the kenotical God in Christianity and the notion of the dynamic *śūnyatā* in Buddhism, then — without eliminating the distinctiveness of each religion but rather by deepening their respective spirituality — we find a significant point of contact at a deeper dimension. This is one of the self-understandings of Buddhism I have arrived at through my dialogue with Christians.

The second issue that has emerged in my understanding of Buddhism through the Buddhist-Christian dialogue is that of Buddhist ethics, especially the problem of justice. How are ethics and the good-and-evil distinction possible in Buddhism, which is based on the notion of emptiness — beyond the good and evil duality? Due to its emphasis on *śūnyatā* and the nondiscriminative mind, is not Buddhism indifferent to ethical issues, especially social evil? Is not Buddhism lacking the notion of justice? To answer these questions, I have been led to clarify the Buddhist meaning of going beyond good and evil and to try to incorporate the notion of justice in the realization of emptiness.

In Christianity, in the light of God, which is love and justice, the distinction between good and evil is clear — and good always has priority over evil. Yet Christianity goes beyond the realm of the ethical and transcends it in the realm of faith because, in the light of God, no one is righteous. No, not one. And we are the foremost of sinners. But we can be saved through faith in Jesus Christ, who is the incarnation of the Son of God. In Christianity, to go beyond good and evil in the ethical sense is to go to God as Absolute Good. In marked contrast, in Buddhism, to go beyond good and evil is the ethical sense is to awaken to *śūnyatā,* which is neither good nor evil. The realization of *śūnyatā,* however, is not indifferent to the distinction between good and evil. Being beyond the duality, beyond good and evil, *śūnyatā* embraces the duality without being confined by it and grasps again the distinction between good and evil in the clear light of emptiness.

In Christianity, love and justice are always linked with one another. Justice without love is not true justice; love without justice is not true love. So love and justice must always be linked together. By contrast, in Buddhism, compassion and wisdom are always connected. Instead of justice, wisdom is emphasized. As a result, Buddhism is rather weak in social ethics and the notions Christians have about solving the problems of society and history at large. How do we interpret this in terms of the Buddhist standpoint of wisdom and compassion? When we do so, Buddhists and Christians will find greater affinity at a deeper dimension and will be able to work together more powerfully in a pluralistic religious situation.

I'd like to talk now about the Buddhist view of history. In the West, it is often said that the Buddhist view of history is not linear but cyclical. So ancient India has no clear consciousness of history; the realization of the directionality of history or the novelty of historical events is not clearly realized in Buddhism or Indian views. This may be so from the Western point of view. If the Western view of history, particularly the Judeo-Christian view of history such as eschatology and so forth, is the only human view of history, Buddhism or ancient India may be said to be lacking this sense of history. But I think Buddhism has its own unique view of history, which is essentially different from the Christian view of history. In short, the Buddhist view of history is neither linear nor cyclical. Time is understood as completely beginningless and completely endless. and if you clearly realize the beginninglessness and endlessness of time and history at this present moment, the whole process of time and history may concentrate into your present existence. In other words, you may embrace the beginningless and endless process of history within your being. This means that eternity is not realized at the end of history — something like the eschatological view — but eternity is realized at this very moment. So the beginning and end of history are also realized at this very moment. We cannot find everything apart from this present moment. How can you find everything apart from this present moment?

Chapter 4

Civilizing the Choctaws: Cultural Expectations and Realities

Clara Sue Kidwell

This paper examines the interaction of Choctaw belief systems and Christian missionary ideas and how differing expectations affected the outcome of federal Indian policy. The response of the Choctaw Indians in Mississippi to Christian missionaries and education constituted a form of adaptation and resistance to white society. It also demonstrates how federal policy failed because of the differing cultural expectations of Indians and whites. History shows us the irony of differing expectations. Actors in situations involving contact between different cultures have culturally based motives, and the responses of their counterparts are not those they expect. The outcomes of differing expectations become apparent in the hindsight of history, and we can examine the discrepancy between intention and result. Although the anthropological concept of acculturation has held that in situations of cultural contact, a less developed group will give up its customs and identity and adopt those of a more advanced culture, history can assess the results of the contact and its impact on both groups.[1]

The experience of the Choctaw Indians in central Mississippi in the early nineteenth century is a prime example of differing cultural expectations, cultural clashes, and adaptation to certain

1. Robert Redfield, Ralph Linton, and Melville J. Herskovits, "A Memorandum for the Study of Acculturation," *American Anthropologist* 38 (1936): 149–52.

aspects of Christianity as a means of cultural survival. The federal government sought to assimilate Indians into American society as farmers so that their hunting lands could be opened to white settlement. The tools of that policy were trade, which introduced Indians to a new economy based on surplus rather than subsistence,[2] and formal education conducted primarily through the agency of Christian missionaries, who attempted to change Choctaw cultural mores and belief systems. There is a certain irony in this use of missionaries as agents of federal policy, given the contemporary emphasis on separation of church and state.[3]

Choctaw leaders adopted education as a mechanism for adapting to the white man's world. They turned mission schools to their own ends, although they differed in their ends and ultimately split tribal members between "Pagan" and "Christian" political parties. The federal government's policy was based upon a distinction between savage and civilized Indians. These categories were based not on religion but on subsistence patterns. The savage Indian hunted in the woods, while the civilized Indian farmed, raised cattle, and became economically self-sufficient. These categories had religious connotations since Americans generally associated farming with the Protestant ethic of using the land to its greatest productivity. The hunter used large tracts relatively unproductively.[4]

The policy of promoting civilization might be rationalized in religious terms as the conflict between Cain the hunter and Abel the husbandman. For the federal officials who began to implement the policy in the first quarter of the nineteenth century, however, religion was not their primary motivation. Thomas Jefferson was inspired by Deistical ideas of human perfectibility to believe that the lifestyles of Indians could be changed to conform

---

2. Richard White, *Roots or Dependency: Subsistence, Environment, and Social Change among the Choctaws, Pawnees and Navajos* (Lincoln: University of Nebraska Press, 1983).

3. Robert F. Berkhofer, Jr., *Salvation and the Savage: An Analysis of Protestant Missions and American Indian Response, 1787–1862* (New York: Atheneum, 1972); Francis Paul Prucha, *Federal Indian Policy in United States History* (Lincoln: University of Nebraska Press, 1981).

4. See Roy Harvey Pearce, *Savagism and Civilization: A Study of the Indian and the American Mind* (Baltimore: Johns Hopkins University Press, 1964), for an excellent discussion of colonial attitudes toward American Indians.

to his ideal of the self-sufficient yeoman farmer. He particularly espoused the distinction between those Indians who could be civilized by education and those who resisted civilization and remained hunters.[5] A growing sense of American nationalism, inspired by the War of 1812, led John C. Calhoun, secretary of war, to declare that "our laws and manners ought to supersede their present savage manners and customs." Indians should be taught the value of individual property and "the common arts or life, as reading, writing, and arithmetic."[6]

The ultimate objective of federal policy was primarily to open Indian land to exploitation by white American citizens. In the land-hungry United States, the government sought to move the savage (i.e., hunting) people to the rich hunting lands west of the Mississippi River, in order to open vast tracts or Indian land east of the Mississippi to white settlement.

The key to civilization in federal terms lay with the self-sufficient, individual farmer. The Choctaws were indeed strong individualists, but not in matters of land, which they held in common. They did have a highly individualistic sense of religion. Men did what they liked because they believed that spirits controlled nature. Each variety of animals and birds had "a great King or presiding Deity" possessed of "great power & wisdom." Men communicated with these spirits through deliberate vision quests, and in a successful encounter, the spirits gave men the capacity for "the most extraordinary works." Having established a spiritual relationship with a bird or animal spirit, a man carried the stuffed skin of its earthly counterpart as a sign of power.[7]

A transcendent power, *Ishtahullo chito,* manifested itself to

---

5. Bernard W. Sheehan, *Seeds of Extinction: Jeffersonian Philanthropy and the American Indian* (Chapel Hill: Published for the Institute of Early American History and Culture at Williamsburg, Virginia, by the University of North Carolina Press, 1973).

6. John C. Calhoun to Henry Clay, Department of War, December 5, 1818, *The Papers of John C. Calhoun,* ed. W. Edwin Hemphill, 19 vols. (Columbia: University of South Carolina Press for the South Caroliniana Society, 1957–), 3:350.

7. Journal of Elliot Mission, American Board of Commissioners for Foreign Missions, Papers, Series 18.3.4, Houghton Library, Harvard University (hereafter cited as ABCFM), vol. 1, folder 1, pp. 7–8; H. B. Cushman, *History of the Choctaw, Chickasaw and Natchez Indians,* ed. Angie Debo (New York: Russell & Russell, [1899] 1962, 92–94.

them "in dreams, in thunder and lightning, eclipses, meteors, comets, in all the prodigies of nature and the thousands of unexpected incidents that occur to man." The term applied both to unusual occurrences in nature and to witchcraft and is probably as close as the Choctaw came to conveying the idea of religious awe or anxiety in the Christian sense.[8]

The supreme Choctaw deity was the sun, and fire was the sun's earthly mate, who communicated information about human activities. The sun guided warriors on the successful warpath. It had the power of life and death, which explains its importance in the funeral customs of the Choctaws. A dead body was exposed to the rays of the sun on a raised platform and allowed to decay, thus giving itself back to the supreme power. After the flesh had decayed, the bone picker was summoned to clean the bones and to preside over a village feast after, as one horrified Frenchman observed, "only wiping his filthy, bloody hands on grass." The bone picker's role in funeral rites and feasting reinforced the integral relationship of life and death.[9]

Choctaw souls were much different from Christian ones. After

---

8. *Ishtahullo* means "anything that excited surprise or suggested a hidden power," and *chito* means "large or great." Cushman, *History of the Choctaw, Chickasaw and Natchez Indians*, 252; Alfred Wright, "Traditions," ABCFM, vol. 3, no. 109; published as "Choctaws, Religious Opinions, Traditions &c." *Missionary Herald* 24 (June 1828): 180–81; John Swanton, *Source Material for the Social and Ceremonial Life of the Choctaw Indians*, Bureau of American Ethnology Bulletin, no. 103 (Washington, D.C. Government Printing Office, 1931), 179.

9. Wright, "Tradition," 196. Although Wright uses the term he in referring to the sun, the Choctaws did not specify gender in pronouns. See Cyrus Byington, "Grammar of the Choctaw Language," *Proceedings of the American Philosophical Society* 11 (1870): 355; John Swanton, "An Early Account of the Choctaw Indians," *Memoirs of the American Anthropological Association* 5 (1918): 65; Cushman, *History of the Choctaw, Chickasaw and Natchez Indians*, 225; Jean Bernard Bossu, *Travels in the Interior of North America, 1751–62*, trans. and ed. Seymour Feiler (Norman: University of Oklahoma Press, 1962), 166–67; William Bartram, *The Travels of William Bartram*, ed. Francis Harper (New Haven: Yale University Press, 1958), 328–29; H. S. Halbert, "Funeral Customs of the Mississippi Choctaws," *Publications of the Mississippi Historical Society* 3 (1900): 353–66; Bernard Romans, *A Concise Natural History of East and West Florida: Containing an Account of the Natural Produce of All the Southern Part of British America in the Three Kingdoms of Nature, Particularly the Animal and Vegetable. Illustrated with 12 Copper Plates and 2 Whole Sheet Maps* (New York: Printed for the Author, 1775), 1:71–72, 82; H. S. Halbert, "Nanih Waiya, the Sacred Mound of the Choctaws," *Publications of the Mississippi Historical Society* 2 (1899): 230; Swanton, *Source Material*, 76–77.

death, a person's *shilombish* (the life force visible in his shadow during life) remained on the earth like a ghost, and his *shilup*, or inner shadow, went to an afterworld, a very beautiful and pleasant land. Only the ghosts of murderers could not find the path and had to spend eternity in a barren place.[10]

Spiritual power was a very personal thing for the Choctaws. Their major public ceremonies were funerals and stickball games, *Ishtaboli*. The games involved teams from neighboring villages, naked except for a belt trailing a horsehair sash, flailing with sticks at a hide-covered ball, attempting to move it to the opposition's goal. As many as one or two hundred men, representing their villages, competed in a contest of village power and prestige, aided by their spiritual leaders, who sang, prayed, and exhorted the players to bring victory to their teams. Winning was not merely a matter of skill and brute force. Villagers danced and spiritual leaders implored the favor of the spirits on their respective teams. The players rubbed their bodies with sacred medicines. Four medicine men smoked to the spirits so that they could judge impartially between the two sides.[11]

Contact with white government agents, settlers, and traders caused conflict with neighboring tribes that could not be resolved in traditional ways. They warred with the Creeks on their eastern boundary, and French and English agents encouraged traditional rivalries and conflicts between the Choctaws and Chickasaws. The Choctaws were allied primarily with the French, and Chickasaws allied with the English.

The end of the French and Indian war in 1763 largely ended French influence among the southeastern tribes, and the British defeat in the Revolutionary War confronted them with American supremacy. In response to these circumstances, the Choctaws signed a series of treaties with the United States government

---

10. Wright, "Traditions," 182.

11. Cushman, *History of the Choctaw, Chickasaw and Natchez Indians*, 184–85; Swanton, *Source Material*, 141–43, 224–25; George Catlin, *Letters and Notes on the Manners, Customs and Condition of the North American Indians*, 2 vols. (New York: Dover Press, 1973), 1:123; Bartram, *The Travels of William Bartram*, 323–24; John Edwards, "The Choctaw Indians in the Middle of the Nineteenth Century," *Chronicles of Oklahoma* 10 (1932): 412–13; Swanton, "An Early Account," 68.

through the early nineteenth century. They ceded parts of their lands, primarily the worn-out hunting lands on their eastern borders and an area along the lower Mississippi. In 1801 at Fort Adams they gave up over two million acres of land along the Mississippi, which would become extraordinarily rich cotton-growing land, in exchange for $2,000 in merchandise and a supply of tobacco.[12] In 1803, they ceded 853,760 acres in southern Mississippi and Alabama, above the boundary with Spanish Florida, in exchange for cloth, rifles, blankets, powder, lead, a saddle and blanket, and one black silk handkerchief. In 1805, at Mount Dexter, they ceded another 4,142,720 acres in southern Mississippi, the proceeds mainly going to pay for trading debts to Panton, Leslie and Company.[13] In 1816 they signed the Treaty of Fort St. Stephen's, giving up part of their eastern territory in exchange for an annuity of $6,000 a year for twenty years.[14] But they protected their hunting lands along both sides of the upper Mississippi River. They maintained their own sense of control over where and how they lived in the early nineteenth century.

As the Choctaw land base shrank, the federal government refined its Indian policy and finally embodied its humanitarian goals in the Civilization Act of 1819, which appropriated $10,000 to prevent "the further decline and final extinction of the

12. Charles J. Kappler, *Indian Affairs: Laws and Treaties*, 5 vols. (Washington, D.C.: Government Printing Office, 1904–41), 2:7–58; Dawson A. Phelps, "Stands and Travel Accommodations on the Natchez Trace," *Journal of Mississippi History* 11, no. 1 (January 1949): 5; John Hebron Moore, *The Emergence of the Cotton Kingdom in the Old Southwest: Mississippi, 1770–1860* (Baton Rouge: Louisiana State University Press, 1988), 9–11; A. J. Pickett, *History of Alabama and Incidentally of Georgia and Mississippi, From the Earliest Period*, 2 vols., 3d ed. (Charleston: Walker and James, 1851, reprinted Arno Press and the New York Times, 1971), 2:234; A. Plaisance, "The Choctaw Trading House — 1803–1822," *Alabama Historical Quarterly* 16 (1954): 393–423.

13. Kappler, *Indian Affairs*, 2:63, 69–70, 87; William S. Coker, *Historical Sketches of Panton, Leslie and Company* (Gainesville: University Presses of Florida, 1976), 22; Arthur H. DeRosier, Jr., *The Removal of the Choctaw Indians* (New York: Harper & Row Publishers, 1972), 29; William S. Coker and Thomas D. Watson, *Indian Traders of the Southeastern Spanish Borderlands: Panton Leslie & Company and John Forbes & Company, 1783–1847* (Pensacola: University of West Florida Press, 1986), 256.

14. *Territorial Papers of the United States*, ed. Clarence E. Carter, 27 vols. (Washington, D.C.: Government Printing Office, 1934–1969), 6:686–87; DeRosier, 37; Kappler, *Indian Affairs*, 2:137.

Indian tribes," and to introduce them to "the habits and arts of civilization." The act authorized the president to employ "capable persons of good moral character," who would teach Indians "the mode of agriculture suited to their situation" and teach their children "reading, writing, and arithmetic." This qualification gave entrée to Christian missionaries as exemplars of "moral character."[15]

But agriculture was really more important to the government than morals, and Andrew Jackson, who was appointed to negotiate a land cession with the Choctaws in 1819, advised John C. Calhoun, secretary of war and the main government official designated to carry out Indian policy, to "circumscribe them, furnish them with instruments of agriculture and you will there by lay the foundations of their civilization."[16]

White civilization had already begun to encroach on the Choctaws throughout the eighteenth century in the intermarriage of Choctaw women and white traders, marriages that produced a growing number of mixed-blood children.[17] By the early nineteenth century, then, a certain element of Choctaw society, white men with Choctaw wives and mixed-blood children, was well aware of the mores of white society. White settlers had introduced domesticated cattle, a major source of change in subsistence patterns, into the nation in the late 1700s, and according to various reports by government agents and missionaries, many Choctaws had given up hunting and had begun to raise cattle, pigs, and chickens. They had always raised corn and beans, and they added melons and cotton to their gardens. In one year the women spun and wove ten thousand yards of cloth, primarily because the deer upon whose skins they had traditionally depended for clothing had been largely hunted out. From a government viewpoint, they were indeed becoming "civilized." Christian ob-

15. U.S. Statutes at Large, III, Chapter LXXXV (March 3, 1819), 516.

16. Andrew Jackson to John C. Calhoun, Nashville, August 24, 1819, *The Papers of John C. Calhoun*, ed. W. Edwin Hemphill, 19 vols. (Columbia: Published by the University of South Carolina Press for the South Carolinian Society, 1957–), 6:270.

17. (Mrs.) N. D. Dupree, "Greenwood LeFlore," *Publications of the Mississippi Historical Society* 12 (1903): 141–52; W. David Baird, *Peter Pitchlynn: Chief of the Choctaws* (Norman: University of Oklahoma Press, 1972).

servers, however, still condemned the savagery of their custom of polygamy and the fact that they had no marriage ceremonies or obvious "exterior worship."[18]

Thus they must still be brought to a state of Christianity. The agents of the government policy of civilization were missionaries of the American Board of Commissioners for Foreign Missions. Staunch Calvinists, coming from the New England bedrock of the Presbyterian Church, they brought with them a cultural understanding of the reality of absolute good and evil, and the conviction that the Choctaws were benighted people who must be brought to salvation through the word of the Christian God. Choctaw leaders, on the other hand, were aware of the need to master the skills of reading, writing, and calculating as a means of dealing with encroaching white settlers and traders (most of whom had little formal education).

The American Board established the first Choctaw mission, Elliot, in 1818. Its stated priority was "securing holiness in the hearts of individuals."[19] Leaders of the Choctaw nation (including a number of mixed-bloods) readily subscribed financial support with the idea that the missionaries would start a school

---

18. John F. Schermerhorn, "Report Respecting the Indians Inhabiting the Western Parts of the United States," *Collections of the Massachusetts Historical Society,* vol. 2, second series (Boston, 1814; Reprinted Charles C. Little and James Brown, 1846), 20–21: Jedidiah Morse, D.D., *A Report to the Secretary of War of the United States, on Indian Affairs Comprising a Narrative of a Tour Performed in the Summer of 1820, Under a Commission from the President of the United States, for the Purpose of Ascertaining for the Use of the Government, the Actual State of the Indian Tribes in Our Country* (New Haven: Published by Davis & Force, Washington, D.C.; Cushing & Jewett, Baltimore; W. W. Woodward and E. Littell, Philadelphia; Spalding & Howe, and R. N. Henry, New York; E. & E. Hosford, Albany; Howe & Spalding, New Haven; G. Goodwin & Sons, Hudson & Co. O.D. Cooke & Sons, Hartford; Richardson & Lord, S. T. Armstrong, Lincoln & Edmunds, Cummings & Hilliard, and G. Clark, Boston. Printed by S. Converse. 1822), 11, 182–83. Morse was commissioned by a missionary group to make a survey of the Indians, and Calhoun supported his trip from the Civilization Fund. See Jedidiah Morse to John C. Calhoun, Washington, February 4, 1820, John C. Calhoun to Jedidiah Morse, Dept. of War, February 7, 1820, *Papers of John C. Calhoun,* 4:634–35, 648–49.

19. American Board of Commissioners of Foreign Missions, *Report of the Committee on Anti-Slavery Memorials, September 1845. With a Historical Statement of Previous Proceedings* (Boston: Press of T. R. Marvin, 24 Congress Street, 1845), 6. Although the quote comes from a later period, in the hindsight of experience, the missionaries still stated a deeply held principle.

for their children.[20] The money came from their $6,000 yearly annuity from their land cession in the Treaty of Fort St. Stephen's (1816). One priority was for blacksmith shops, which would meet a very practical need to adapt to the new technology required for farming.[21]

Finances gave Choctaw leaders power in their relationship with the missionaries. Money gave them the opportunity to make demands on missionaries for schools in their districts and near their homes. Cyrus Kingsbury, head of the American Board mission, resented those demands. His priority was converting the Choctaws to Christianity.[22] The American Board, however, did not have the human or financial resources to meet all the Choctaw demands, and Kingsbury feared that his inability to do so would destroy whatever influence he could muster among the tribe's leaders.[23]

The Choctaw leaders had great faith in education, but they rather quickly began to reject the missionary style of teaching, which involved physical discipline and manual labor, Christian ideals that were very foreign to Choctaw child-rearing practices. One Choctaw complained that the school at Elliot was in session only two or three hours a day and that the missionaries "made little boys work with heavy axes & when they had lame feet."[24]

Differing cultural expectations were also apparent for children in the American Board schools. The Calvinist theology espoused by the Presbyterian missionaries who were its agents

20. Kingsbury to Samuel Worcester, French Camps, August 9, 1819, ABCFM, Series 18.3, vol. 2, folder 31.

21. John McKee to John C. Calhoun, Choctaw Agency, June 10, 1819, National Archives, Letters of the Secretary of War, Received, roll 2, frame 1263.

22. Journal of Elliot Mission, June 21, 1822, ABCFM, vol. 1, folder 5.

23. Calhoun to Kingsbury, Department of War, November 7, 1820, *Papers of John C. Calhoun,* 5:428; Kingsbury to Worcester, Pigeon Roost, Jan. 2, 1821, ABCFM, vol. 2, folder 72.

24. Robert Cole was the son of a Chochumma woman and a white man. The Chochummas had been wiped out by Choctaw and Chickasaw attacks, and Cole's mother had evidently been adopted into the Choctaw tribe. See "Journal of Proceedings," Case no. 2, National Archives, Record Group 75, Choctaw Removal Records, Entry 275; H. S. Halbert, "District Divisions of the Choctaw Nation," *Publications of the Alabama Historical Society, Miscellaneous Collection* 1 (1901): 377; Journal of Elliot Mission, August 3, 1821, ABCFM, vol. 1, folder 2; Journal of Elliot Mission, May 28, 1822, ABCFM, vol. 1, folder 5; Journal of Elliot Mission, June 9, 1821, ABCFM, vol. 1, folder 1.

placed power in the hands of God to inspire the anxiety about one's soul that was a hallmark of salvation. When individuals began to question their destiny and their own behavior, it was a result of the operation of God's will upon them. One such instance of anxiety among the students at Elliot was John Long, who was discovered in his room weeping bitterly. He expressed his feelings "that I am a sinner and every thing that I do is displeasing to God. I wish that the missionaries would pray for me in case I die and go to hell and be tormented forever."[25]

Such distress and feelings of subservience were, however, quite foreign to the autonomy and personal freedom afforded Choctaw children and adults. Choctaw child-rearing practices stressed love, affection, and modeling of adult behavior rather than punishment. Choctaw men had access to spiritual power through vision quests and dreams in which they established reciprocal relationships with spiritual forces. They had the power to affect the outcome of their activities through those relationships. The gulf between Presbyterian theology and Choctaw beliefs was profound.

The missionaries turned to the use of the Choctaw language as a means of educating children in order to better Christianize them. They translated various biblical texts into Choctaw and devised such things as spellers and arithmetic books for use in their schools.[26] If language was to be a tool of civilization, however, the objectives of its wielders were different. Byington saw written Choctaw as "an instrument in the hands of the Lord of communicating...a knowledge of his salvation." David Folsom, a prominent mixed-blood leader, hoped that "if his warriors could read thus he could introduce laws among them to much better advantage."[27]

---

25. Journal of Elliot Mission, April 18, 1821, ABCFM, vol. 1, folder 3.

26. The first book published in Choctaw was a spelling book that appeared in 1825. Alfred Wright and Cyrus Byington, *A Spelling Book, written in the Chahta Language, with an English Translation: Prepared and Published Under the Direction of the Missionaries in the Chahta Nation, with the Aid of Captain David Folsom, Interpreter* (Cincinnati: Published by Morgan, Lodge and Fisher for the Missionary Society, 1825). See James Constantine Pilling, *Bibliography of the Muskhogean Languages* (Washington, D.C.: Pilling, Govt. Print. 3ff., 1889), for a list of extant early Choctaw texts.

27. Byington to Evarts, Gibeon, September 2, 1826, ABCFM, vol. 3, folder 78;

At least one Choctaw accepted some aspects of Christianity on his own terms. Tunupinchuffa related an experience to Loring Williams, one of the American Board missionaries. He was out hunting when he saw a deer lying by the side of the road. He said to himself that perhaps his "Heavenly Father" meant it for his use. If it were still there when he came back with a rifle, it would be a sign that God gave him the right to kill it. When he returned, the deer was still there, and Tunupinchuffa killed it and returned thanks to "my Father above."[28] Traditional Choctaw beliefs were that animals gave themselves willingly to be killed if the hunter were properly respectful and properly purified. The skill of the hunter was a result of spiritual relationships and power acquired in a vision quest. The distinction that begins to blur in Tunupinchuffa's account is that between a gift bestowed by an omnipotent deity and a kill dependent on the hunter's proper relationship with his prey and the spirit world.

Some Choctaws adopted Christianity, but missionaries despaired at the small number of their converts. As they labored, white settlers were appropriating Choctaw lands west of the Mississippi. There are three crucial treaties that affected the relationships between Choctaws and missionaries between 1820 and 1830 — the Treaty of Doaks Stand in 1820, the Treaty signed in Washington in 1825, and the Treaty of Dancing Rabbit Creek in 1830. In 1820, despite the school at Elliot and other signs of growing "civilization," the Choctaws were still being pressured by the federal government to cede their land in Mississippi and move west. Andrew Jackson, the chief government negotiator, told them that they had more land than was necessary for farming, but too little game to live by hunting. "The Choctaw nation must dwindle to nothing" unless they would take the western lands the government offered in exchange for their lands in Mississippi. Those who wished to remain in Mississippi could take individual allotments and live under the protection of the federal

Byington to Evarts, Aikhuna, July 7, 1826, ABCFM, vol. 3, folder 77; Byington to Evarts (extract), Aikhunna, July 1, 1826, ABCFM, vol. 3, folder 76.

28. Loring S. Williams to Jeremiah Evarts, Aiikhunnah, May 4, 1829, vol. 3, folder 61, ABCFM, Series 18.3.4.

government, and fifty-four sections of their ceded land would be sold to raise money for schools.[29]

In 1825, the Choctaws negotiated another treaty, this time ceding part of their lands west of the Mississippi River that had been occupied by whites. Again, education was one of the bargaining points. The Choctaws asked for $9,000 annually for twenty years for "mechanical institutions," and the same amount for the education of Choctaw children in "colleges or institutions out of the nation." They flattered James Monroe that by acquiring "a knowledge of literature and the arts," the Choctaws would be able "to tread in those paths which have conducted your people . . . to their present summit of wealth & greatness."[30] What they finally got was $6,000 a year for twenty years to be applied to education in "the mechanic and ordinary arts of life."[31]

The treaty sharpened the split between the mixed bloods of the tribe, the major supporters of the mission effort, and Mushulatubbee, the last of the full-blood traditional chiefs. Mushulatubbee, chief of the Northeast District of the nation, committed the total allocation for schools to the Choctaw Academy in Kentucky, a school ostensibly supported by the Baptist Church but whose curriculum was actually quite secular. It included reading, writing, arithmetic, grammar, geography, astronomy, vocal music, and, on a rather ironic note considering the future outcome of Choctaw land claims, practical surveying.[32] Mushulatubbee's support of the Choctaw Academy was symptomatic of

---

29. Kappler, *Indian Affairs*, 2:193.

30. Calhoun to Choctaw Delegation, Washington, November 9, 1824; Choctaw Delegation to Calhoun, Washington, November 12, 1824; Calhoun to Choctaw Delegation, Washington, November 15, 1824; Calhoun to Thomas H. Williams and Christopher Rankin, November 15, 1824; J. L. McDonald to Calhoun, Washington, November 16, 1824; Calhoun to Choctaw Delegation, November 19, 1824; David Folsom and J. L. McDonald to Calhoun, Washington, November 20, 1824; Choctaw Delegation to Calhoun, Washington, November 22, 1824; Calhoun to Choctaw Delegation, November 27, 1824; David Folsom and J .L. McDonald to Calhoun, November 30, 1824, *Papers of John C. Calhoun*, 9:374–75, 379–80, 383–84, 384–85, 388, 390–91, 397–99, 407, 411–12. See also *American State Papers*, 2 Indian Affairs, vol. 2, 554–55. An account of the negotiations is also given in Herman J. Viola, *Thomas L. McKenney Architect of America's Early Indian Policy: 1816–1830* (Chicago: Sage Books, Swallow Press Inc., 1974), 124–34.

31. Kappler, *Indian Affairs*, 2:212.

32. Shelley D. Rouse, "Colonel Dick Johnson's Choctaw Academy: A Forgotten Educational Experiment," *Ohio Archaeological and Historical Quarterly* 25,

his disdain for the American Board schools and missionaries. Although they had tried to start a school at his home at his request, Mushulatubbee continued to drink with his captains in defiance of missionary teachings, and his wife ordered the teacher around in a way that the missionaries found unacceptable.[33]

The slow progress of conversion and incidents of Choctaw recalcitrance counterbalanced the evidence that the Choctaws were giving up hunting and embracing farming and education. Thomas McKenney, head of the Office of Indian Affairs in Washington, expressed growing disillusionment about the effects of the civilization policy. He had traveled through the southeast in 1827 to try to convince the Choctaws and Chickasaws to move west, and he had seen their situation firsthand. He asked, *"What are humanity and justice in reference to this unfortunate race?"* Should they remain in "a wretched and degraded existence," surrounded by a white population "whose anxiety and efforts to get rid of them are not less restless and persevering, than is that law of nature immutable which has decreed that under such circumstances, if continued in, they must perish?"[34]

McKenney's disillusionment was fed by the report of one Choctaw that some of the American Board missionaries were "inefficient, bigoted, or overzealous" in their efforts, and perhaps also by criticism of his own management of the office.[35] A more powerful voice was Andrew Jackson's. He appealed to "humanity and national honor" to save the Choctaws, Chickasaws, and Creeks by moving them west. The white population, with its "arts of civilization," had destroyed "the resources of the savage" and thus had "doom[ed] him to weakness and decay."[36]

At its heart, however, Jackson's policy was driven not by hu-

no. 1 (January 1916): 97; Carolyn Thomas Foreman, "The Choctaw Academy," *Chronicles of Oklahoma* 6 (1928): 460.

33. Cyrus Kingsbury to Jeremiah Evarts, June 7, 1824, ABCFM, vol. 2, folder 128, Kingsbury to Evarts, Mayhew, July 19, 1824, ABCFM, vol. 2, folder 133.

34. Thomas L. McKenney to P. B. Porter, Dept. of War, 1828, *New American State Papers, Indian Affairs,* 13 vols. (Wilmington, Del., Scholarly Resources, Inc., 1972), 1:73.

35. J. L. McDonald to Tho. L. McKenney, Jackson, Miss., April 25, 1826, NA-OIA-LR, M234, roll 69, frames 326–29; Viola, 193.

36. Andrew Jackson, First Annual Message to Congress, James D. Richardson,

manitarian concern but by his own commitment to maintaining the integrity of the American nation. His objection to Indian tribes was that they were essentially sovereign nations within American territory. Jackson believed with an almost religious fervor that American territory was sacrosanct. If Indian nations remained as separate entities within American states, they undermined that integrity. Choctaws believed, with similar fervor, that their homeland in central Mississippi had been given to them through the religious sanction of spiritual powers.[37] If earlier American ideals of national identity and later idea of "manifest destiny" assumed an almost mystical dimension in American history, certainly the beliefs of Choctaws are understandable.

Federal pragmatism began to reject the idea of "civilization" as a means of assimilating Indians. Andrew Jackson had been elected president of the United States in 1828, and he pushed through Congress the Indian Removal Act of 1830, which embodied his ideal of the integrity of the American nation and the dependent status of Indian tribes. Its implications were clear. For the Choctaws, their transition to a settled, agricultural way of life and their support of formal education could not protect them from the overwhelming momentum of white settlement and westward movement. For the American Board, their schools had failed to achieve either widespread Christian conversion or significant literacy among the Choctaws, things which might have been taken as signs of civilization.

The board had established schools at thirteen locations between 1819 and 1830 and served approximately fifteen hundred students, although the actual number of children educated is difficult to estimate because it is hard to tell how many of the count for each year were returning students.[38] The largest schools

---

A Compilation of the Messages and Papers of the Presidents, 1789–1897, 10 vols. (Washington, D.C.: Government Printing Office, 1899), 3:1021.

37. See Michael Paul Rogin, *Fathers and Children: Andrew Jackson and the Subjugation of the American Indian* (New York: Alfred A. Knopf, 1973), for a discussion of Jackson's motives with regard to the Indian Removal Act of 1830. See H. B. Cushman, *History of the Choctaw, Chickasaw and Natchez Indians* (Greenville, Texas: Headlight Printing House, 1899), for Choctaw origin traditions.

38. 22d Congress, 1st Session, House of Representatives Document No. 194, Board of Commissioners — Foreign Missions, Memorial of the Prudential Com-

were in neighborhoods dominated by mixed-blood families. The missionaries were unwilling to venture into the strongholds of traditional Choctaw culture.[39] Leaders who represented the traditional culture of the tribe, Mushulatubbee and Robert Cole, rejected the board's efforts to start schools near their homes, despite their initial requests. The rejection was as much political as cultural, but it nevertheless undermined the board's position.

In 1830, when the Treaty of Dancing Rabbit Creek was signed, there were 528 students in American Board schools, 278 at the schools associated with mission stations, and 250 in Choctaw villages, but only 299 were full-blood Choctaws.[40] Although the

---

mittee of the American Board of Commissioners for Foreign Missions, Respecting the Property of the Board in the Choctaw Nation, April 2, 1832, p. 3.

39. *Missionary Herald* 20, no. 1 (January 1824): 3; George S. Gaines, "Reminiscences," *Alabama Historical Quarterly* 24 (Fall and Winter 1964): 158; American Board of Commissioners for Foreign Missions, *Monthly Paper* no. 3 (June 1823).

40. This number included only 67 new students. American Board, *Monthly Paper*, 11–12; American Board of Commissioners for Foreign Missions, *Report of the American Board of Commissioners for Foreign Missions, Read at the Twenty-Second Annual Meeting, Which was Held in the City of New Haven, Conn., October 5, 6, and 7, 1831* (Boston: Printed for the Board by Crocker and Brewster, 1831), 104. Taking the potential school-age population of 6,375 children under the age of ten from the total population, enumerated in the federal census in 1831 at 19,554, and including an additional 4,630 males over sixteen (although the missionaries generally discouraged parents from sending older boys, who caused the greatest problems and complained the most), the school population in 1830 was only 5.3 percent of the total. As a comparative measure, there were fourteen schools among the white population of the state of Mississippi by 1830, although statistics are not readily available on the number who attended. See Aubrey Keith Lucas, "Education in Mississippi from Statehood to the Civil War," in Richard Aubrey, editor, *A History of Mississippi*, 2 vols. (Hattiesburg: University & College Press of Mississippi, 1973), 1:356. For their educational achievements, 36 were learning to spell in English, 36 were studying English reading lessons, 63 read in the English Testament, and 58 in the English Reader, and 57 could write in English; 126 read in Choctaw and English, 90 spelled and 245 read in Choctaw only, 12 composed in Choctaw only, 11 wrote in both Choctaw and English, and 137 could write the language; 51 studied arithmetic, 64 geography, and 22 grammar. American Board, *Monthly Paper*, 12. The number of conversions reported by the board was also minuscule compared with the total population. Churches were organized at Elliot, Mayhew, Bethel, Goshen, and Emmaus. At Mayhew and its outlying stations, Aiikhunna and Yoknokchaya, 284 persons had become members — 8 blacks, 20 whites, and 256 Choctaws. About 50 had become members at Goshen, and about 40 at Emmaus. About 360 people belonged to the churches in the Choctaw Nation by the end of 1831, and the number of children baptized was 244. American Board, *Monthly Paper*, 11–12; American Board of Commissioners for Foreign Missions, *Report of the American Board of Commissioners for Foreign Missions. Read at the Twenty-Third Annual Meeting Which was Held in the City of New York, October 3, 4, and 5, 1832* (Boston: Printed for the Board by Crocker and Brewster,

Choctaws wanted education as a way of dealing with the non-Indian world around them, they were largely unwilling to accept the schools of the American Board. As long as they maintained political autonomy, they tried to use schools for their own ends. What history, shows, however, is that as strong as culturally based responses of Indian tribes may have been to white society in the early 1800s, the American perceptions of Indians as savages were appropriated into the political agenda of American society in the early nineteenth century, and despite Indian attempts to understand and deal with the culture of the white population that was rapidly surrounding them, the cultural assumptions of American society about Indian savagery and degradation overwhelmed the strategy of Choctaw leaders to adopt education as a means of adaptation to changing circumstances and the very immediate changes in Choctaw subsistence patterns that were going on.

The Treaty of Dancing Rabbit Creek in 1830 marked a fracturing of the nation, with the capitulation of a group of Choctaw leaders to federal pressure to leave their homeland in the southeast. Despite the incredible hardships of a forced removal, the Choctaws reestablished their nation in the Indian Territory in the early 1830s, and by 1851, Cyrus Kingsbury reported that they were a largely Christian nation.[41]

The missionaries of the American Board entered the Choctaw nation with faith in the power of preaching and education to change the lifestyles of the natives and lead to their salvation, but they made several crucial mistakes. They allied themselves primarily with the mixed-blood element of the tribe and alienated at least two full-blood leaders who might have given them access to native communities. They subjected their pupils to physical discipline and labor that was at odds with traditional Choctaw child-rearing practices, thus stirring up discontent. Their schools

---

1832), 104; Kingsbury to Calhoun, Mayhew, Choctaw Nation, Oct. 1829, ABCFM, vol. 3, folder 41.

41. Henry C. Benson, *Life Among the Choctaw Indians, and Sketches of the South-west* (Cincinnati: Published by L. Swormstedt and A. Poe, for the Methodist Episcopal Church, 1860; reprinted New York: Johnson Reprint Corporation, 1970), 28; *Memorial Volume of the First Fifty Years of the American Board of Commissioners for Foreign Missions* (Boston: Published by the Board, 1861), 259.

became pawns in power struggles among political leaders. They remained underfunded by the government and the board, and they never could muster the personnel and financial support to extend their efforts throughout the Choctaw Nation. By 1861, the American Board admitted, with regard to its efforts, that

> the object, with most of the parents, was not the spiritual good of their children, but their social and material elevation; ... the patrons of the missions were impatient for the civilization of the Indians, and would not give them time.[42]

The conflicting motives of Choctaws and missionaries undermined the ability of both to achieve their ends, and federal policy makers took the perceived failure of the Choctaws to adopt Christianity and education as a rationale for Indian removal. Resistance to a federal policy so deeply embedded in cultural assumptions about civilization could not save the Choctaw homeland in Mississippi.

---

42. *Memorial Volume*, 321.

Chapter 5

Religious Conflict

Samuel Ruiz García

I would like to thank the Parliament of World's Religions for my invitation to speak to this respectable assembly about religious conflict. In fact, I had thought that in Christianity, and perhaps in all the religions of the world, some conflicts existed; but, as I started to reflect on this topic, the same thing happened to me as the character in G. K. Chesterton's *The Ball and the Cross,* who, being a scientist, hated the Cross as a symbol of conflict and who began to find crosses everywhere: the fences in the fields, the branches of the trees, the intersections of roads. In this same way, I began to see many conflicts in religion, even to the point of becoming a bit crazed and saying now that religion *is* conflict and that there would be no religion if no conflicts existed. Either it is mankind who, in the midst of its conflicts, searches for the Divinity, or it is the Divinity who searches out mankind in its debility.

The newborn infant announces its presence by challenging the cosmos with an existential scream: the infant begins its life because it begins to cry. The physical and psychological growth process is no more than a series of responses to the different challenges of life: walking, talking, eating, the search for sustenance, being conscious of one's life, loving in the midst of suffering.

Human relations between individuals, groups, and races are relationships full of conflicts, to which are given good or bad treatment and without which there would be no history, nor human growth.

Salvation History

Each member of the human race carries within him- or herself the seal of conflict. We all experience in our own flesh, what Saint Paul said in his letter to the Romans: "I do not the good that I wish, but the evil I do not wish, that I perform" (Rom. 7:19). As created beings, our existential limitation puts us in conflict with the eternal dimension; tied down by the bonds of our mortality, we aspire to the possession of wisdom and we realize that each day we know more about less. Our condition as created beings overrides our unlimited aspirations. In summary, we can encompass all of what has been said in a phrase that is the cornerstone of all religions: we aspire to the divine, aware that we are sinners. The cosmos itself directed *teleologically* toward God, is subjected by injustice and evil to a profound deviation from its ultimate purpose, the glory of God.

If we had thought of the way in which salvation should have taken place, we would never have thought of bringing it about, by means of the conflict of the cross which is symbol and synthesis of failure. "For our sakes, He made Him to be sin who knew nothing of sins" (2 Cor. 5:21). "For the foolishness of God is wiser than men, and the weakness of God is stronger than men" (1 Cor. 1:25).

This whole story was preceded by the conflict of constructing a nation with a handful of slaves freed from Egypt: Yahweh chose them as his preferred ones, even though they were a hard-headed people, and gave them the Decalogue that dignified them as a nation even as they transgressed it.

Christianity and Spain's Conquest of the New World

It was economic factors that marked the evangelization of the new world: finding the shortest way from Spain to India in order to lower the cost of marketing spices. And once the new world was discovered in this way (which is the reason we are called Indians), the sword and the cross joined together to bring about a political and spiritual servitude of the conquered. The honest narrations of these same invaders can't hide the shame of the massacres, the greediness for precious metals, and the enslaving eagerness that the altar of production be served by extending the enslavement to vast regions of Africa. The forced enlistment of the Indians with their respective owners, so that they would render greater productivity and profits for the owners, was justified by also acquiring the "pious" obligation of teaching them the faith. Evangelization of the Indian was dishonored with their unmerciful exploitation, with plundering and robbing of the productive profits of New Spain, with the increase of taxes for the Crown and with the large profits for the *encomenderos* who were those that had the large land grants, which included the Indian inhabitants.

And, although in justice we have to separate from all of this the abnegated and well-intentioned work of some of the missionaries, in the judgment of the Indian existed the contradiction in having to accept a belief in the Lord and Creator of life, preached by those who destroyed life. For this reason our Bartolomé de las Casas, the first bishop of Chiapas, asserted that the conversion of the Indians was a miracle against nature, asking, "How could they believe in God who is giver of life, but who is preached by those who terminate life?"

Another underlying conflict within the conquest of New Spain is the strengthening of the emerging capitalism in the old world. While other countries (including England) augmented their economic and political power by dominating Africa and India, Spain was able to excel mainly due to the exploitation of the gold and silver mines, which caused numerous Indian miners' deaths. On this point, a Guatemalan Indian prince commented that the eyes of the Spanish shone with the color of the gold and the silver and that even while asleep they shouted, "Gold! Gold! Gold!"

Bartolomé de las Casas commented in his "extremely brief narration of the destruction of the Indians":

In the midst of these tame sheep [the indigenous peoples]...
the Spanish came...as very crude wolves and tigers and lions, who had been hungry for many days. And they haven't done anything else but to mangle them, kill them, distress

them, worry them and destroy them. The reason that the Christians have killed and destroyed so many important things (animals and plants) and such an infinite number of "souls," has been solely for having as their driving force, gold and the accumulation of riches in a few days and to rise to high positions, which their person doesn't merit; in other words, for the insatiable greed and ambition which the Christians have had.

Taking from the Indians their land and submitting them to inhuman demands of work were the determining factors in a production favorable to the interests of the empire, which, together with the system of taxation, precipitated an unjust accumulation of riches, which helped Spain cure the wounds of the Muslim penetration in its territory. At the same time, it offered Spain the opportunity to present all of this, as zeal for spreading the faith and for augmenting the Kingdom of God. It makes the blood boil to read the pseudo-pious reports of the viceroys of the king, some of whom were clerics, who requested the intervention of the king in the correction of the cruel treatment of the Indians by some authorities, using as their sole reason for asking for his mediation that the extreme mistreatment caused so many deaths and, therefore, a scarcity of workers, and consequently less profit for the landowners and fewer taxes paid to the king.

It is not at all strange that the first bishop of Chiapas condemned the conquest itself and the unjust accumulation of goods with fiery statements, predicting any number of disasters for Spain, if it did not withdraw from the land it had snatched away from the legitimate owners. Even though he could not accomplish all that he had intended, at least his life, dedicated to the defense of the Indian, had a beneficial influence in the "Law of the Indians." However, for having denounced the abuses, he caused himself to be discredited as the creator of the "black legend."

The Evangelization of Latin America

Aside from the social and political conflicts of the conquest of New Spain, the cultural and religious conflict endures even today.

Having extended Christianity throughout the Roman Empire, the initial conflict started when the Christians, who came from throughout the empire, were required to take on the Judaic law with all of its consequences. The conflict was resolved by recognizing that the Judaic law had already expired. Only for the sake of unity was obedience to some external signals demanded. In this way, Christianity was able to incarnate itself in the Roman Empire, and thus began what is today called Western Christian culture. The Spanish conquest brought the Christian religion, identifying it, in its practices, with Western culture.

We can understand the anguish of those first missionaries who encountered great numbers of "pagans" whom they felt they had to baptize, since it was a accepted, that "outside the Church there was no salvation." In this way, "a religious sandwich" was generated, since no interreligious dialogue between representatives of Christianity and their counterparts of the indigenous religions took place.

A religious blend was the direct result. Traditional religious concepts took on Christian forms of expression; Christian ideas are thought about and lived from the perspective of the indigenous religions; indigenous religious rites are carried out secretly and thus a religious schizophrenia is born in the continent.

In this way, the demand made on the Indians was that in order to be Christians, they had to stop being themselves; that is to say, they had to abandon their own identity in order to become human and Christian, according to cultural molds that were totally foreign to them. Since there was nothing more than "obscurity of error and the shadows of death" outside of Christianity, it was not possible to recognize in the indigenous religions any type of values which could have been the basis of a minimum of interreligious dialogue.

On the other hand, the age-old cultures and values transmitted from generation to generation tell us that they are worthy of great respect. What is more, in the case of the American Indian cultures, their religious values are the nucleus which unifies and holds together the whole culture. If the conversion process implicitly requires the abandonment of the "pagan" religion, in order to accept Christianity, this same conversion process would imply nothing less than the destruction of the culture itself. In other words, the plundering of their land and riches is aggravated by the stripping away of their identity.

With this understanding we can ask ourselves: In what would consist the evangelization process today? Would it consist in resurrecting the pre-Spanish cultures? That would be archaeology rather than evangelization. Or would it be the total respect of the cultures in an attitude of contemplation? But that would not be being sent to announce the kingdom of God. Or because of the transcendent destiny of humankind, is it necessary to destroy all cultures in order to construct a universal and unique culture? Then why did God permit various cultures and, in fact, send his Son to incarnate himself in a particular subculture of the Roman Empire? In the end we are left with the question, what is evangelization?

In the Second Vatican Council, by demand of the African bishops, this question was given profound thought. God has permitted that each people have its own way in which his redeeming presence is manifested. In answer to the search of humankind he reveals himself and makes himself present in one, unique history of salvation. God, having permitted that each people have their own redeeming experience, in the fullness of time, manifests himself by means of Jesus Christ, who calls all peoples and races to construct a New People, or in other words, a People of peoples. In this way, in contrast to the Jewish people, who were chosen as an ethnic group, the new People of God is a universal People, in which each one contributes their own salvation history, as it has been lived out, uniting it with the richness of the other salvation histories. The universality of this New People and their unity assume these differences in an integrated whole. Thus the unity is not uniformity but rather differences held in communion.

For that reason we recognize the presence of God in the heart of all cultures, and we discover, as an integral part of evangelization, the announcement of this divine presence which makes itself visible in the ethical and religious values of the different peoples. (The Second Vatican Council calls them "Seeds of the Word," following the example of the church fathers.) These values should be complemented in an interchange with the Christian experience.

In this way, a dialogue with the African and Indian cultures of
this continent could be initiated, one which should have been initiated five hundred years ago. The Indian as well as the African
cultures of this continent are called to reflect on what the Gospel proposes from the point of view of their culture and with
their own means of reflection. This is not Thomistic philosophy
nor any of the modern philosophies, but rather their own means
of reflection. In this reflective process the message will be incar-
nated in the culture and give rise to different native churches,
"sufficiently established and gifted with their own energy and
maturity, sufficiently prepared with their own hierarchy, united
with the faithful, and with the appropriate means to carry out
a completely christian life" (Vatican II, *Ad Gentes* 6 par. 3).
"In this missionary activity, in the preaching of the Word and
in the celebration of the sacraments, whose center and crest is
the Holy Eucharist..., whatever truth and grace were already
present in the nations like a quasi-secret presence of God, are
liberated from malignant contagion and restored to their author
Christ... whatever good is found planted in the heart and mind
of the people or in their own rites and cultures, not only does
not perish, it is purified, elevated and consumed for the glory of
God" (*Ad Gentes* 9 par. 2).

After five hundred years of being crushed in every way, the
African and Indian communities of the continent emerge having
repossessed their consciousness of their cultural identity and of
their capacity to contribute their values, which are fundamental
to their cultures, to the construction of a new world. This indigenous theological reflection, which has taken place in a lapse
of less than three years, is manifested in the reflection which
has been done by the Indians of the pre-Spanish religions (so
that there can be an interreligious dialogue) and those of the
Christian faith with their very own cultural instruments. In this
reflective process of dialogue, Christianity shares its faith experience and the perception of God's plan for humanity, but it
also embraces the age-old religious experiences, in which God
has made himself present, thus enriching its own experience of
church.

The Option for the Poor

Another, apparently wider-spread conflict exists which continues to shake us up even today: it is the relation between religion and the poor.

Our conception of the way society is constituted has given us the impression that the value of the individual, the social class, or the country is founded in a practical hierarchical order in which what is possessed determines who that person, class, or country is. In other words, "having more" is the same thing as "being more." Those who do not have education, economic resources, or the possibility of ascending the social strata are totally irrelevant in the social struggle, or those who have nothing are simply considered as the "masses" or as a number. Those who are economically nonproductive, whether they be children or the elderly, do not fit into this social system, and their brutal elimination tends to justify itself legally.

The Christian religion disconcertingly (to our bewilderment) puts the socially marginated and the exploited at the very center of human and religious life. Not only are those who have nothing the parameter within which the social and religious life should be regulated, but God defines himself as the God of the poor. Jesus, being the only one who could make a choice about where and when to be born, chose to incarnate himself in margination and poverty, as the road to redemption. What is more, Christ gives due place to the poor as a visible sacrament of our salvation, because Jesus identifies himself with them. At the final judgment at the end of time, our conduct will be measured according to how we have or have not recognized Christ in the hungry, the thirsty, the naked, the imprisoned (Matt. 25:35–36).

In the Second Vatican Council Pope John XXIII understood the urgency of revising the duties of the Catholic Church, according to the historical situations of the present moment. Before an active or applied atheism, how can God be announced? How can we respond to the new historical situations from a faith perspective? It was not a matter of only methodological changes or linguistic changes, but rather a case of the householder who brings forth from the knapsack of the Good News, new things as well as the old (Matt. 13:52). This could not be done effectively without the testimony of a Christianity, if not united, at least searching for unity. For that reason the council affirmed the saving presence of God in history and recognized the validity of other Christian experiences with which we have a tie that is stronger than our differences. But, a few days before the opening of the council, Pope John XXIII made known a third enlightening point: "The Church, in its relation with the developing nations, discovers what it is and what it should be: the Church of the poor, that is, the Church of everyone." In these words there is a great depth: clearly he is speaking of the relation of the Church with structural poverty (in other words, "the developing nations"). The same statement affirms that this relationship between the church and structural poverty is the parameter which determines the very essence of the church itself ("what it is and what it should be"). It is understood that no relationship is static; rather it is a revisable, dynamic process. Pope John XXIII affirmed that there is no contradiction in the church of the poor being the church for everyone. Moreover, the church could not be the church of everyone if it did not situate itself and put down its roots in the lowest level of society. To do otherwise it would be a dominating church which imposes from above, and not a church which questions all, as did Christ, from the perspective of the poor of Yahweh.

Even though this "enlightening point" of John XXIII was present throughout the documents of the Second Vatican Council, it could not be a pivotal point as were the other two for the simple reason that, at that time, Europe was just beginning to experience poverty with some Third World immigrants from Asia and Latin America, and thus the consequent theological reflection was still lacking. As Cardinal Giovanni Battista Montini (later Pope Paul VI) pointed out in the conciliar meeting room, it was not a matter of treating the topic of the church where the poor were spoken of, but rather to speak of the poor was to speak of the church, and, if this was not done, it was impossible to speak of the other two enlightening points (dialogue with the world and ecumenism).

When the bishops of Latin America returned from the council they felt that the three "enlightening points" needed to be rethought from within the Latin American reality. Theoretical or (for that matter) practical atheism was not a problem in our continent where the majority of the people profess Christianity (whether they practice it or not). That is to say, more than having "nonbelievers," we have "nonpersons." A road to the unification of Christians, rather than being thought to consist of agreements and convergent theologies among ourselves, was found in commitments to liberation. Meanwhile, the reflection about the church and its relationship to the poor brought about the meeting in Medellín. Colombia, in 1968, in which we discovered ourselves as a church tied to the structures and men of power; and from there we went on to discover our complicity with the dominant structures. As a result the Latin American church proclaimed a conversion movement, its rejection of unjust structures, and its option for the poor as evangelically obligatory.

In this way, we discovered once again that "happy are those who know they are spiritually poor: the Kingdom of heaven belongs to them!" (Matt. 5:3; Luke 6:20) and that what we do for the poor, Christ will judge as done for him. We rediscovered that the Gospel is Good News for the poor, that to announce the Reign of God is to announce and undertake in each epoch the liberation of the poor; that the poor should be creators of their own history and that they, who are the preferred of the Lord, can also evangelize us. Even more so, we rediscovered that on the shoulders of the poor rests the responsibility to announce and contribute to the construction of the Reign of God and in that way, with the help of God, to generate a new society for the same people who are their oppressors and enemies, thus being, at the same time, unifying elements.

For that reason a church that opts for the poor needs to go through a conversion process to make itself a church with the poor and, definitively, a poor church. As the bishops said at their conference in Puebla, Mexico, in 1979:

> The church should revise its own structures and the life of its members, especially of its pastoral workers, looking for an effective conversion. This conversion in itself requires an

austere life-style and a total confidence in the Lord, since the evangelization activity of the Church will count more on its way of being and the power and grace of God, than it will on "having more" and secular power. Thus it will present an image of being authentically poor, open to God and to its brothers and sisters available, and where the poor have a real capacity of participation and are recognized for their value. (Puebla 1157–58)

Progress and the Reign of God

Everything we have been saying is the basis of the conflict between religion and progress; not in the sense in which it was spoken about in times past of a church which disturbed progress because it lived the hope of a celestial future and condemned material values while affirming the supremacy of the spirit; nor, although it is positive in a certain way, in the sense of Karl Marx, who considered religion "the opium of the people" because it helped in their alienation to avoid a collective suicide.

As it can be defined today, the conflict between religion and progress is in the destructive and oppressive conception of what social progress is and its consequences: on the one hand, such a concentration of economic and political power that it brings with it death to the poor; meanwhile, on the other hand, it does such violence to nature with its irrational growth that it irreversibly destroys the habitat of the human species.

Technology, progress, and the societal model that grows out of them have combined today, in contemporary history, to generate death: 95 percent of the world's total income is concentrated in 25 percent of the world's population; thus there is 5 percent of the income to be distributed among 75 percent of the population. This means that with this particular social system, the more success it has, the further it gets from satisfying the most basic need which it contends is its reason for being: satisfying hunger. In this way, the cry for justice rises up from within this same social system and from nature itself, whose destiny has been changed by mankind and is suffering because it has been violently dominated by the sinfulness of mankind. The just perceive this and would like it to change: they feel their impotence and at the same time do not even know what to do nor how to ask for help. However, the Holy Spirit is in the center of their hearts, praying from their innermost selves with unutterable groanings to the Father who, since he is God, can understand (Rom. 8:18–27).

For that reason, the conflict appears today when out of religion arises the proposition of a social system where the poor would be the measure of the rights of the rest of society; a proposal in which society would be structured with mechanisms for distribution and sharing, not for concentration and accumulation. It would be the permanent establishment of the "year of grace" which Jesus announced to his people in the synagogue (Luke 4:19). Every seven weeks of years (every fifty years), the Israelites celebrated a jubilee year, which was a year of social readjustment in which all debts were pardoned and houses and land were returned to their original owners so that there would be no Pharaohs in the midst of the people. This jubilee year was declared by Jesus to be the constant task of the Christian.

But our society does not walk along this path. The Free Trade Agreement among Canada, the United States, and Mexico (NAFTA) has already had its consequences. In Mexico the number of families that receive 70 percent of the national income has fallen from fifty to twelve, while the world of poverty has grown. The measures taken to comply with the demands of foreign debt lead to death, for example, through the reduction of medicines and medical services to isolated locations. Meanwhile some loudly proclaim what others think but don't dare say aloud: they decree the death penalty for all those who are not covered by the salvific mantle of the laws of the marketplace, outside of which there is no possibility of salvation in history.

The Conflict between Religion and Liberation

If we take a good look at history, the liberating transitions that have taken place have had to pay the price of violently let blood: a measure which arises out of a consciousness of being oppressed and which, because of that consciousness, articulates in organized ways, in civic and political movements or organizations.

The existent oppressive system invariably responds with calculated measures to put down the civic and political movements or organizations: bribery, surveillance, intimidation, repression, imprisonment, torture, and death.

On not a few occasions, religion has formed part of the thinking which justifies this type of state or society. In that case, religion is just another piece of the dominant system's puzzle, a part of the superstructure. The process of education, both formal and informal, leads individuals to an acritical submission to the existing social system. The massive media communications select happenings and reread them and publish them in the light of the interests and conveniences of the system. A set of "pseudo-values," generally accepted as necessary, is proclaimed so it can form a part of the society; this even includes which human rights are to be respected and who enjoys these rights.

But the Christian does not adjust him- or herself to these outlines. Christianity is not a religion in which man looks for a God who measures up to human desires. Christianity is, rather, a liberating irruption of God in history, in a history in which the Son of God takes on flesh to make of humankind children of God.

Consequently, Christianity, by nature, is in opposition to all types of slavery. Since God is "the God of the poor," Christianity takes in its hands the cause of the enslaved and works for their liberation (cf. Isa. 61:1, 41:17; Ps. 140:13; Luke 6:20). This liberation, for the Christian, does not include armed violence as a liberating instrument; the Christian moves him- or herself within the framework of the commandment of love, which includes loving one's enemy as Christ taught with his word and his example (Matt. 5:44; Luke 6:27, 35). The impoverished have on their shoulders the responsibility to transform society, not only for their own benefit, but also for the benefit of their enemies since they are also equally, to some extent, victims of the oppressive system. The Christian should have clearly in mind what Paul says: "Do not let evil defeat you, conquer evil with good" (Rom. 12:21). The only thing the Christian cannot accept, without letting go of being a Christian, is hate.

But, who doesn't see the conflict that this presents? The dominant system itself is (and openly manifests itself as such, with a thousand and one justifications) institutionalized violence which generates death: the repressive violence of imprisonment, torture, and death. And while an organization or movement with legitimate demands is repressed with armed force, at the same time, ethically it is not allowed the possibility of armed resistance to this repression unless the following conditions exist:

- That the violations of fundamental rights are in truth that, and are grave and prolonged.

- That all the peaceful recourses have been tried.

- That worse disorders are not provoked.

- That there is reasonable hope of success.

- That it is not possible to reasonably foresee other solutions.

When the bishops of Nicaragua, in a collective pastoral letter to all Christians, indicated that it was not against their faith or the Gospel to participate in the Sandinista movement, which was already in its armed stage, they had read the above-mentioned conditions and ascertained for themselves that, in that moment in history, the Reign of God would not be constructed with the government of Somoza but could be with Sandinism.

The Intraecclesial Conflict of Christianity

Some of the worst conflicts existing within, above all, the Catholic Church today are those that refer to its hierarchical and not democratic character, the lack of liberty of opinion in regard to the affirmation of its dogmas and the situation of oppression and disequality that women experience in the church.

By nature the church is hierarchical. Christ chose his apostles in order to send them in his name to announce his Kingdom to the ends of the earth. It was not they who chose Jesus; rather, as he said, "You did not choose me; I chose you, and appointed you to go and bear much fruit, the kind of fruit that endures" (John 15:16). The power with which he sent them forth is a power which is exercised as service. Jesus said to them: "The kings of this world have power over their people, and the rulers are called

'Friends of the People.' But this is not the way it is with you; rather, the greatest one among you must be like the youngest, and the leader must be like the servant" (Luke 22:25–26; Mark 10:42–43). For that reason, if, in faithfulness to its constitution the church maintains its hierarchical character, it is in order to assure, inasmuch as is possible, service to the ecclesial and human community, so that it is as free as possible from political events and occasions. It is a hierarchy instituted to promote democracy (Medellín, p. 173, no. 17).

This is a conflict which has a certain artificiality to it, since all institutions (and even more so, all religions) have their transcendent points which are never negotiable. With the exception of these nonnegotiable points, there should be room for opinion about any number of other points which are reflected upon naturally in the light of fundamentals of the faith.

What we must admit is that lately, at certain levels of our Catholic Church, there has been unwarranted supervalorization of the role of pontifical teaching, without a theological analysis which distinguishes what is an affirmation of faith, what is theological reflection, what is opinion within the church, what is utilization of the socioanthropological sciences, and what is simply subject to opinions. As a lamentable expression of human deficiency, we could even speak of a repression within the church which, in the name of discipline, carries out theological coercion.

It is surprising that even those political governments which wanted to establish a theoretical and practical equality of men and women within their social framework did not obtain total success; this shows us a tremendously introjected, and therefore, transmitted and inherited, male dominance in society.

The influence which the Jewish tradition has had, historically and culturally as preparation for the coming of Christianity, has immersed within it a social reality in which "women and children are not counted"; genealogies were always constructed following the paternal lineage. It is strange that we give the name "matrimony" (and not patrimony) to the institution of the family, given that woman is perceived as purely receptive to a masculine action of which the woman suffers the consequences of genetic evolution, birth, education within the house.

There is evidence that a healthy evolution of humankind is taking place in which women are recuperating, with fatiguing work, their rights which had been usurped and are acquiring equal treatment; sadly, in the juridical structure of some religions, there has not been a correspondent recognition of these advances. It would seem that participation in the church and in its decision-making processes is given only as alms to women.

The biggest difficulty in our church is in relation to the ordination of women as priests. On both sides of the argument, the discussion revolves around the understanding of what Jesus did: if he chose men apostles because of cultural norms or because of a theological principle which holds that this ministry should reflect Christ's will that the priesthood participate in, as well as, represent him in his role as Head of the Church specifically as man because he chose to become man and Son of God (and not woman and daughter of God). But at the same time, we cannot ignore the privileged situation of Mary, who, for being chosen to be the mother of Jesus, will be called blessed by all generations (Luke 1:48).

Conclusion

With all that has been said, we can see that our topic is not how to resolve or confront the ever-emerging conflicts of history, but rather how to assume them as part of our journey.

I believe that we have to accept that conflict is the law of life; that without conflict we would not mature humanly nor would we clarify our own religious positions; and that many conflicts will someday appear as essential aids in our definition of ourselves individually and collectively in history. There is where Christ the Lord, promised to send his Spirit so that those things which we can not now understand will be understood in all their truth when he, the Spirit of Truth, comes.

Chapter 6

Religion and Globality: Can Interreligious Dialogue Be Globally Responsible?

Paul F. Knitter

The title of this working session, "Religion and Globality," could well serve as the subtitle for the 1993 Parliament of the World's Religions. A quick run down the list of major presentations, lectures, seminars, and workshops makes clear how dominant among participants is the concern to relate religion to what the official parliament brochure terms "the critical issues facing humankind." These issues are spelled out concretely in the brochure: "Nonviolence and Peace, the Earth, Social and Economic Justice, the Human Community, Science and Technology, Politics and Liberation." Our parliament is inspired and directed by the conviction that religious concerns *must* be related to such global concerns; one of the central goals of the parliament is to call religions together so that, having *come* together, they might *act* together in addressing these global needs and crises.

One might say that the two dominant themes of the parliament are *dialogue* and *global responsibility*. The two must be linked. Interreligious dialogue must be globally responsible; it must have as its context and content the "critical issues" that are teasing and torturing humanity and the planet. And global responsibility, as Hans Küng has been stating, cannot be carried out unless religions make their joint contribution.[1] This sense of having to

---

1. Hans Küng, *Global Responsibility: In Search of a Global Ethic* (New York: Crossroad, 1991).

join dialogue and global responsibility flows out of a dual awareness which more and more religious persons are experiencing and responding to: an awareness of the *religious Other* and of the *suffering Other*. To be a religious person today requires one to relate one's own religious identity to the identity of other religious persons and to the identity of others who are suffering. Other persons who are religious in ways different from our own and other persons or beings who are suffering because of their social or economic or ecological situation — these two Others today confront and challenge anyone who would call her- or himself religious. This challenge derives from the multitude of these others — so many religious Others and so many suffering Others stare me in the face and ask me what my religious faith has to say to them.

What our parliament is sensing and expressing is that, somehow, one's religious responses to both these Others must be a shared response; that is, to address one, I must address the other. To effectively address the suffering Others, I must address my fellow religious travelers in other traditions; and to carry on a meaningful dialogue with other religious persons, I must listen to the voice of the suffering Others. Again, we conclude that dialogue and global responsibility, or religious pluralism and eco-human well-being, must go together.

I say *must* go together. But there are many who would warn that to link religions and globality, or interfaith dialogue and a commitment to human and ecological justice, is a very difficult, dangerous, perhaps even impossible task. I'm referring to what is called nowadays the postmodern criticism. Our postmodern consciousness warns us of the dangers of all universalizing programs, of trying to set up any kind of "common ground" between differing cultures or religions. Every universal claim or program, we realize, is usually, if not always, my own particular view of things, limited by my own perspective and probably geared to promote my own needs or power. In other words, the postmodern critique warns us that what we think is necessary may be impossible — you can't link a diversity of particular religions with a universal globality! As soon as you call for or impose "globality" you are going to smudge or suffocate particularity.

Let me spell out the difficulties more clearly: Is an inter-

religious dialogue that calls all participants to be globally responsible and concerned about human and ecological well-being
something that *all* religious traditions can affirm? Or is such an
approach to dialogue once again another camouflaged maneuver
to control the discourse with a Christian or a Western agenda?
When we dramatically invoke such terms as *global responsibility*
or *liberation* or *justice* as the context or goal for the dialogue,
can we be sure that these notions will be understood in basically
the same way by all the participants in the conversation? In other
words, using the title of Alasdair MacIntyre's book, *Whose Justice?*[2] or *whose* well-being, are we talking about anyway? Isn't
this whole proposal for a globally responsible or justice-centered
dialogue just another attempt (at best naive, at worst calculating)
to fashion the Golden Calf of an absolute norm or foundation
before which believers of all traditions must now bow? Doesn't
"global responsibility" or "social justice" or "ecological sustainability" now become the absolute, final norm for all truth — all
the more idolatrous and pernicious when it is *my* understanding
of justice or sustainability that functions as the final norm?

These are the issues I will try to explore in this working session. I'd like to suggest why and how linking interfaith dialogue
and global responsibility is not only a necessity but also a very
real and promising possibility. In the first part of this presentation, I will try to show that the very nature of religion and
religious experience, as we view it in its many-splendored forms,
indicates that all (or at least "most") religious traditions have the
capability, if not the established record, of affirming global responsibility as ground and goal for interreligious encounters. As
I will argue, this capability is all the more enhanced today when
our earth, in both its sufferings and its newly discovered mys-
teries, is becoming a locus for shared religious experience and
vision. Following that, I will take up the sticky question of how
"justice" or "well-being" can serve as a universal criterion for
truth without becoming a new foundational or absolute norm for
truth — how justice can be an ever-reliable counselor who helps

---

2. Alasdair C. MacIntyre, *Whose Justice? Whose Rationality?* (University of
Notre Dame Press, 1988).

us but who never lets us off the hook of having to make our own decisions.

Global Responsibility —
Can All Religions Endorse It?

From both what we can see in the world of religions, and from what the academicians tell us, religion, in all its exuberant forms, has to do with changing this world for the better. Yes, religion has to do with what is called God or the Ultimate, and with life after death, and with altering or expanding our consciousness — but it also has to do with confronting, specifying, and then repairing what is wrong in the way human beings live their lives together in this world. Whether you call it evil or ignorance or incompleteness, there is something wrong with the state of the world as it is, and religion wants to do something about it. In some way, every religion wants to "make better" or "heal" or "get beyond" what is not right or working in society and the world. In other words, some form of what we might call *soteria* or salvation (well-being) is envisioned and sought after.[3]

Speaking from an Asian perspective, and from a broad knowledge of Asian religions, Aloysius Pieris believes that all religions, in various forms, take their origins from some kind of a primordial liberative experience. The symbol of a "liberating Spirit," Pieris feels, is appropriate. Differing religions can be seen as various languages which give polyphonic voice to this liberating Spirit: "[E]ach faith is a language of liberation, that is to say, a specific way in which the Spirit speaks and executes its redemptive intention in a given cosmic-human context."[4] Pieris recognizes that this Spirit as symbol is open to a broad interpretation: "The 'Spirit' could be understood as the human or the divine Spirit. In nontheistic religions such as Buddhism, Jainism, or Taoism, it stands for the *given* human potentiality to speak,

---

3. Gordon D. Kaufman, *The Theological Imagination: Constructing the Concept of God* (Philadelphia: Westminster Press, 1981), 197–99.

4. Aloysius Pieris, "Faith-communities and Communalism," *East Asian Pastoral Review* 3 and 4 (1989): 297.

to seek, and find total human liberation."[5] He also points out what is so evident in the religious world today — that what is primordial can become lost and therefore have to be retrieved: "[R]eligion is *primordially* a liberation movement, if seen in the context of its origin, though it does tend *subsequently* to be domesticated by various ideologies; that is to say, religion ever remains *potentially* liberative, even if *actually* subservient to non-liberative structures."[6]

Religion, therefore, calls on what is more than human (at least the human as we now experience it) in order to transform or liberate the human. In the words of V. Harvey, "[W]hen we call something religious we ordinarily mean a perspective expressing a dominating interest in certain universal and elemental features of human existence as those features *bear on the human desire for liberation and authentic existence.*"[7] To transform the human context will mean, generally, to oppose or resist the forces that stand in the way of change or newness. Thus, David Tracy, ever cautious about general statements regarding religions, can recognize:

> Above all, the religions are exercises in resistance. Whether seen as Utopian visions or believed in as revelations of Ultimate Reality, the religions reveal various possibilities for human freedom.... When not domesticated as sacred canopies for the status quo nor wasted by their own self-contradictory grasps at power, the religions live by resisting. The chief resistance of religions is to more of the same.[8]

---

5. Ibid.

6. Ibid., 296.

7. Quoted in David Tracy, *Dialogue with the Other: The Inter-Religious Dialogue* (Grand Rapids: Eerdmans, 1990), 54. Emphasis mine.

8. David Tracy, *Plurality and Ambiguity: Hermeneutics, Religion, Hope* (New York: Harper & Row, 1987), 84. Therefore, according to Raimon Panikkar, to even raise the question whether religion has anything to do with changing this world is to fall victim to a dualism that runs contrary to the ideals of most, if not all, religions. It is a dualism between God and the world, or religion and politics, that stems not from the content of religious experience but from external efforts (especially in the West) to spiritualize or privatize religion and thus dilute its political power (Raimon Panikkar, "Religion or Politics: The Western Dilemma," in *Religion and Politics in the Modern World*, ed. Peter H. Merkle and Ninian Smart [New York: New York University Press, 1983], 52). Gandhi, then, was right when he announced: "I can say without the slightest hesitation and yet in all humility that those who say that

The Mystical Prophetic Dipolarity of all Religion

Naturally, in claiming that all religions are world-oriented and
bear an energy that can change the earth, I am not saying that
this is all they contain or that this is their only concern. Besides this world-transforming energy, there is another category of
power that is just as important. Scholars have spoken of both
the *prophetic* and the *mystical* power of religion. But they have
used these categories to divide religions vertically, one from the
other. Thus they have distinguished the Abrahamic religions of
the West from the Indic religions of the East. According to this
division, Judaism, Christianity, and Islam are prophetic religions
involved in the world; Hinduism and Buddhism are mystical religions calling their followers to disengage from the world and
explore their own inner depths.[9] What I am suggesting, however
(and here I am following the lead of scholars who know Asian
religions much more deeply than I do),[10] is that these differences
between the prophetic and the mystical do not run vertically
between religions but horizontally within them.

In each religious tradition we can find both mystical and
prophetic experiences and visions. And the line between them
is not so much a wall that separates as a bond that unites
and mutually nourishes. So we must admit and encourage the
mystical-prophetic dipolarity that vibrates and flows back and
forth within our own and all religious traditions. This dipolar energy of religion animates a twofold project, each aspect essential,
each calling to and dependent on the other: to transform both
the within and the without, to alter inner consciousness and social consciousness, to bring about peace of the heart and peace

religion has nothing to do with politics do not know what religion means" (*My
Autobiography* [Boston: Beacon Press, 1957], 504). Or maybe they know very well
what it means, but seek to deny or stifle the power of religion.

9. Hans Küng, *Christianity and the World Religions: Paths of Dialogue with
Islam, Hinduism, and Buddhism* (New York: Doubleday, 1986), 174–77.

10. Stanley Samartha, a Christian surrounded by Hindu neighbors, chides his fellow Christians and reminds them that such neat classifications between mystical
and prophetic religions "need to be corrected. Very often the manner in which such
observations are made and the conclusions drawn are historically untrue and theologically wrong. To perpetuate this notion would amount to bearing false witness
against our neighbors." "Religions and the Aspirations of the People," *Religion and
Society* 30 (1983): 113.

in the world, stirring the individual to an earnest spiritual praxis and also to a bold political praxis.

The dynamic and call of this mystical-prophetic dipolarity is what tells Christians that they can love God only when they are loving their neighbor, or Buddhists that wisdom is not possible without compassion, or Hindus that the yoga of knowledge or devotion must be combined with the yogas of action in this world. Neither the mystical nor the prophetic is more fundamental or more important; each calls to, and has its existence in, the other.

Certainly the dipolarity, or the balance, will be maintained differently within different religions, or within different denominations of the same religion, or at different stages within an individual's personal journey. Frequently — all too frequently — the balance is not maintained; and then we have mystics whose spirituality becomes self-indulgent, insensitive, or irresponsible; or, we have prophets whose actions become self-serving, intolerant, or violent. When the mutual feedback system between the mystical and the prophetic within a religion breaks down, the religion becomes either an opium to avoid the world or an indult to exploit it.

So today, "In all the major religious traditions, there is a search for new ways to unite those mystical and prophetic trajectories."[11] In an age in which we are horrifyingly aware of human and ecological sufferings, and of the devastating dangers seeded within this suffering, every religion is being challenged to rediscover the prophetic power of its tradition and to unite it to the mystical. The prophetic power is there, perhaps beneath a mystical overgrowth, perhaps hidden in narratives and symbols which spoke to a different age and which are in need of revisioning for this age. If this power is not tapped or refurbished, the religious tradition will lose its ability to speak to and engage the many persons today who feel the prophetic challenge of our suffering world.

---

11. David Tracy, "God, Dialogue, and Solidarity: A Theologian's Refrain," *Christian Century*, October 10, 1990, 900.

A Shared Diagnosis and Remedy
for the Human Predicament

But we can go a step further. As we survey the vast terrain of religious history and experience, we can identify, I suggest, not only an undercurrent of concern for transforming this world, not only a dipolar flow between mystical and prophetic experience, but also an analogously similar *diagnosis* of what is wrong with our world and a *prescription* for what must be done to fix it. The operative word in that last sentence is "analogously." I am not suggesting that all the religions of the world are really proposing identical or essentially similar soteriologies — programs for how the world and we humans are to be "saved." Rather, my experience in interreligious dialogue and social action (an experience shared by many others, I suspect) has been that when one plunges into the vast diversity of religious analyses of what is wrong with the human predicament and how it might be set right, when one wrestles with the very real and powerful *differences* in these analyses and programs, one finds that the differences one is wrestling with turn out, for the most part, to be friends rather than foes.

More specifically, it seems that the analogous similarities between the differing religious views of humanity's fundamental problems take shape around the issues of the *nature of the self* and how the self can be understood or experienced differently. According to the myths, doctrines, and ethical admonitions of most religions, humankind's woes flow from a pool of disunity and disease fed by a false notion of the self; to remedy the situation we must dry up or replace the contents of that pool. The problem, in other words, has to do with the way we understand and live out our sense of who we are. Either we understand ourselves incorrectly, or our "selves," in their present state, are corrupted or incomplete. In each case, something has to happen to the self, either notionally or really. We either have to understand or experience ourselves differently, or our "selves" have to be infused with new or healing energies. Whether the fix is cognitional from within or ontological from without, it has to lead to a different way of acting in and of relating to the world around us.

So the problem recognized analogously by different religions has to do with separation or selfishness; and the remedy has to do with relationship and mutuality. In many different ways, most (all?) religions seek to convert the energies of one's self from a centripetal to a centrifugal movement and so to broaden the focus of concern from not only me or us (egocentricity) to Other or others (altruism). We have to find our "selves" outside of ourselves; to realize who we are, we have to experience ourselves as part of something that is greater than what we understand ourselves to be right now. John Hick, using Western terminology, seeks to summarize all this by describing the analogously common goal of most religions as a shift from self-centeredness to Reality-centeredness.[12]

Admittedly, as feminist critics point out, such ideals of a self-less self have been fashioned by patriarchal religions — that means, by men whose primary "sin" has been an inflated self that abuses other selves, and not by women whose primary sin has been a deflated self that allows itself to be abused by others. Thus, what I am proposing here as a diagnosis common to all religions requires a feminist hermeneutics of suspicion that will assure that the selfless self does not become the enslaved or subordinated self.[13] Still, I think feminists would agree that the "saved self" or new self is one that is sustained in the web of mutuality rather than in the cell of egocentricity.[14]

Thus, Sallie King appeals to this transformed self in her response to the postmodern argument that because all experience is socially constructed it is impossible to know if there is a common mystical core within all religions.[15] She grants that it is impossible to get at this core by simply comparing what the different tradi-

---

12. John Hick, *The Interpretation of Religion* (New Haven: Yale University Press, 1989), 299–309.

13. Valerie Saiving, "The Human Situation: A Feminine View," in *Womanspirit Rising: A Feminist Reader in Religion,* ed. Carol Christ and Judith Plaskow (San Francisco: Harper & Row, 1979), 25–42; Judith Plaskow, *Sex, Sin, and Grace: Women's Experience and the Theologies of Reinhold Niebuhr and Paul Tillich* (Lanham, Md.: University Press of America, 1980), 51–94.

14. Catherine Keller, *From a Broken Web: Separation, Sexism, and Self* (Boston: Beacon Press, 1986).

15. Such an argument is offered in Steven T. Katz, "Language, Epistemology, and Mysticism," in *Mysticism and Philosophical Analysis,* ed. S. T. Katz (New York: Oxford University Press, 1978), 22–74.

tions *say* about it; a comparative analysis of "Nirvana" or "God" or "Tao" or "Dharma" gives us no assurance that they all have a common reference point. But if we look at how persons *feel* and especially at how they *act* after they have undergone some form of mystical experience, we can talk about the likelihood of something in common, even though we can never define it. All mystical experience, it would seem, brings about a new sense of self, or what King calls a new "existential grounding" for the self. There is a "radical transformation of the experiential self sense, a radical axiological and existential grounding."[16] The self finds itself rooted and animated in something that is broader than the ego-self, something that connects it with other selves and with the world.[17]

Here, as they say, a "reality check" is necessary. To hold up the transformation of the hide bound self into the other-oriented self as a diagnosis and remedy common to most religions is to hover in the realm of *religious ideals* — what the religions generally preach. It is not their historical track record — what they often do. Such discrepancies, persistent throughout religious history, must be admitted. There is within every religious tradition what Paul Tillich has called "the demonic" — the possibility, indeed, the propensity, to be turned in the direction opposite the other-oriented vision of its founder or original witness. Within the heart of every religious body there dwells not only Dr. Jekyll but Mr. Hyde, not only "the culture of utopian peaceableness" but also the "culture of violence and war."[18] In our postmodern consciousness, we realize, perhaps more clearly than ever, that the religions' vision of selfless love and liberation has been turned into the ideological weapons of dominance and conflict. And so I

16. Sallie King, "Two Epistemological Models for the Interpretation of Mysticism" *Journal of the American Academy of Religion* 56 (1988): 275.

17. This appeal to how people feel or act provides the basis for a corrective response to the emphasis that Joseph DiNoia places on the diversity of religious views of salvation. His emphasis is so heavy that it seems to exclude any genuine possibility of analogous similarities such as Hick and Tracy are proposing. See Joseph DiNoia, "Pluralist Theology of Religions: Pluralistic or Non-Pluralistic?" in *Christian Uniqueness Reconsidered: The Myth of a Pluralistic Theology of Religions*, ed. Gavin D'Costa (Maryknoll, N.Y.: Orbis Books, 1990), 118–34.

18. Elise Boulding, "Two Cultures of Religion as Obstacles to Peace," *Zygon* 21 (1986): 502.

make this claim for a common diagnosis with a sense of realism and sorrow, and with a conviction of the need constantly to call religions to live up to their ideals.

The Earth: Common Ground for Encountering the Sacred

So far, our proposal has been that differing religions can and must share a global responsibility for eco-human well-being and justice. Even though many contemporary scholars are extremely uneasy with such a universal proposal (and would want to cut it up into socially constructed pieces), I think that global responsibility enables religious persons to take an even bolder step. In this section I would like to explain why I, along with others (whom I shall be referring to), am convinced that the kind of global responsibility we have been talking about can be not only a shared commitment but also a *shared context for religious experience,* feeding and reforming our different religious traditions. Global responsibility is not only an *ethical task* that all religious persons can take up together; it can also be a *religious task* and a source of shared experiences by which believers from different communities can better understand and communicate each other's religious stories and language.

Let me try to clarify what I mean, without watering it down. The challenges that face us in our suffering brothers and sisters and in our suffering planet are calls to all religious persons to be not only *prophets* transforming the system but also *mystics* plumbing the depths of the Divine or the Real. To feel global responsibility, to give oneself to the task of struggling for *soteria* in this tormented world, to join hands with victims and to experience victimization in the struggle for justice, to feel claimed by the sacredness of the earth and called to protect the earth — such human experiences and activities constitute a universally available locus, an arena open to all, where persons of different religious backgrounds can feel the presence and empowerment of that for which religious language seems appropriate.

Yes, the language will be different. Yes, there will be many other ways in which the Transcendent can touch us or explode within our consciousness. Still, I think we can all recognize that to respond to the sufferings of our fellow sentient beings is an undertaking in which we ourselves are taken under and claimed by something that is more than what we are or that goes beyond our everyday awareness. Working for eco-human justice becomes a common context in which we find ourselves using our different religious stories and symbols. So our experiences of injustice are as different as our languages, but at the same time, these differing words are flowing from a common experiential process. There is, I daresay, something "common" within the diversity. We are "communing" with that which sustains or might be the goal of our various traditions. Working together for justice becomes, or can become, a *communicatio in sacris* — a communication in the Sacred — available to us beyond our churches and temples. But just how does this work?

Extra Mundum Nulla Salus — Outside the World No Salvation

Edward Schillebeeckx helps us understand how global responsibility can be a "communication in the Sacred" when he takes the long-standing ecclesiocentric dictum, "Extra ecclesiam nulla salus" (outside the church there is no salvation) and turns it on its head to read "extra mundum nulla salus": outside the world there is no salvation. Here Schillebeeckx is not just speaking to his fellow Christians but is announcing a reality that he feels can be recognized and affirmed by all religious persons. It is precisely in the confrontation and struggle with a world littered with limitations and inadequacies (to put it philosophically), or with suffering and injustice (to put it existentially), that we can, and do, encounter the Divine. Again, his language is Christian, but the experience he is describing can, I believe, be caught and illuminated by a variety of religious symbols and narratives.

Schillebeeckx describes a basically identical worldly process in which many people, from a variety of religions and cultures, find themselves today. They encounter situations of "negative experience of contrast" before which they find themselves pronouncing, first, a spontaneous and forceful no to what the situation is, and then a resolute yes to how it might be transformed. In this explosive no and then in this determined yes, we find the first stirrings of religious experience — what Schillebeeckx calls "pre-religious experience": these are "important human experiences, namely, negative experiences of contrast: they form a basic human experience which as such I regard as pre-religious experience and thus a basic experience accessible to all human beings, namely, that of a 'no' to the world as it is."[19] The no doesn't just stand there. Spontaneously, it gives birth to a yes by which persons are claimed and called to resist and reform what is before them:

> The fundamental human "no" to evil therefore discloses an unfulfilled and thus "open yes" which is as intractable as the human "no," indeed even stronger because the "open yes" is the basis of that opposition and makes it possible. ...Both believers and agnostics come together in this experience. That is also a rational basis for solidarity between all peoples [we can add, all religions] and for common commitment to a better world with a human face.[20]

This "natural" or "given" human response of resistance leading to hope and action is the raw material, as it were, out of which religious experience or faith can take form. This is what Schillebeeckx means by "no salvation outside the world": it is in the confrontation with and struggle to improve the world that the reality of the Transcendent/Immanent makes itself felt. For Schillebeeckx, the praxis of involvement in the world has a primacy in religious experience and in what Christians call revelation:

> Revelation presupposes a process meaningful to men and women, an event that already has relevance for them and liberates them, without direct reference to God, *etsi Deus non daretur* [as if God didn't exist]. What is decisive is the good action which brings liberation, without which religious nomenclature becomes this, a meaningless facade and

---

19. Edward Schillebeeckx, *The Church: The Human Story of God* (New York: Crossroad, 1990), 5.
20. Ibid., 6.

redundant superstructure.... Only in a secular history in which men and women are liberated for true humanity can God reveal his own being.

Salvation from God comes about first of all in the worldly reality of history, and not primarily in the consciousness of believers who are aware of it.[21]

These are strong statements, perhaps too strong. The emphasis on this-worldly, prophetic involvement seems to exclude other forms of religious experience. Remove their exclusive tones, however, and they still make a positive assertion that can, I trust, be taken seriously by persons of different religious traditions: by first "feeling" the presence and power of something more in our efforts to overcome the "negative experiences of contrast" we know what we are talking about when we use our religious language. Here the experience is illuminating the language and the language is forming the experience; there is a nondual reciprocity between the two. Religious language such as "truth" or "love" or justice" — or "Dharma" or "Tao" or *karuṇā* — takes on new or added meaning and power in both identifying and expanding what we have already felt in our struggles to pronounce our no and remain faithful to our yes.

The struggle to overcome the reality of suffering and injustice not only provides us with the experiential "receptors" with which we can use and understand religious language; it also brings about within us an existential process which, as I suggested earlier, can be found, in various garbs, within most religious traditions. In the usually complex and painful effort to speak a no to suffering and carry out a yes to transforming this world, our individual selves are deconstructed. We find the center of gravity in our lives shifting from our individuated self to other selves and, even, to a broader Reality. We are *decentered* and so refocused. Jon Sobrino describes this process as he has seen it take place among many of his companions (some of them martyrs) in El Salvador: "This de-centering of oneself, this transfer of one's ultimate concern from oneself to the life of the poor, redounding as it does to the attainment of one's own life as well, is the

---

21. Ibid., 12.

subjective experience of the holy. It may be that, at the level of formulation, one cannot go much further. Words may seem insufficient."[22] This experience of losing-gaining oneself, of becoming a no-self/trueself, is a commonly described quality of religious experience in most traditions. Sobrino says it can happen outside the monastery or temple and in the impoverished villages or ravaged rain forests, amid all cultures and religions.

My suggestion, therefore, is that just as persons from various spiritualities have sought a multifaith *communicatio in sacris* — a sharing of religious experience — in ashrams, monasteries, and participation in each other's meditational or prayer practices, so today they can also share their religious experiences and language in the concrete praxis of a global spirituality and the struggle for eco-human justice that such responsibility demands. We can commune in the sacred as we commune in the sufferings of our world. Thus, a group of sixteen representatives of various religious paths in India could conclude their dialogue with this joint statement:

> When we stand for justice and freedom and for people's right to life with dignity, we stand for those realities and values, in terms of which *all faiths image the Mystery of the Divine.* . . . The downtrodden people with their history of hope and struggle is the *locus*, the place, of authentic encounter with God. In confronting injustice and working for a new India, a new world, where people are equal and free, and where resources are for all, there exists a profound spirituality even if it is not recognized, made explicit.[23]

The Earth: A Common Story for Sharing Particular Stories

But there is another way — broader and both more challenging and promising — in which globality, or our world as it is, can provide common ground for interreligious dialogue. As a num-

---

22. Jon Sobrino, *Spirituality of Liberation: Toward a Political Holiness* (Maryknoll, N.Y.: Orbis Books, 1987), 110.

23. Final report of the consultation organized by the Indian regional committee of EATWOT, Febuary 27–March 2, 1989 in Madras. Privately distributed.

ber of contemporary scientists, philosophers, and theologians are urging, today the earth is providing us not only with a context for experiencing the Divine/Truth in a vast variety of ways but also with a *common story* by which we can better understand our different religious experiences, link them, and give them some unified shape. All these thinkers — better call them visionaries — are seeking to understand religious phenomena in relation to scientific and ecological phenomena. I'm referring to theologians with dirty hands and earthy hearts such as Thomas Berry, Sallie McFague, Charlene Spretnak, Jay McDaniel, Rosemary Radford Ruether, and to scientist-philosophers such as Brian Swimme, Fritjof Capra, and Charles Birch. If I can bring their various concerns and claims into a focus, it would be something like this: given what we *know* about how the universe came about and how it functions, and given what we *have done* to our earthly corner of the universe, today the earth itself, providing our place within and scenic view of the universe, offers all humans (that means all cultures and all religions) a *common cosmological story.*

This story, as people are trying to tell it today, has two facets. As a *religious story,* it tells us who we are and how we can find the Truth that religions seek; it provides us, in other words, with a cosmological myth in which we can understand our individual myths. As an *ethical story,* it provides us with general, but still usable, norms for adjudicating the truth claims that we as human, especially as religious, beings find ourselves making. Briefly, let me try to describe the content and functions of this common cosmological story.

A common religious story: "For the first time in our history, we have empirical evidence for a common creation story." So declared a group of fifty representatives from a variety of religious traditions in what they called "An Earth Charter," prepared by the International Coordinating Committee on Religion and the Earth for the Earth Summit in Rio de Janeiro, June 1992.[24] They were announcing on the international level what some theolo-

---

24. The document was distributed by the International Coordinating Committee on Religion and the Earth, Wainwright House, 260 Stuyvesant Ave., Rye, NY 10580.

gians have been saying among themselves and their communities: science, in what it tells us about how the universe originated and how it works, is providing all religions with a *common creation myth*. What Thomas Berry and Brian Swimme call "The Universe Story" can function as a transcultural religious story.[25]

In drawing on the findings of science, these theologians are not seeking to resolve the religion versus science debate; they are not concluding that science finally has proved the existence of God or established the validity of a religious worldview. Rather, these theologians are suggesting that if religious persons will listen to — or "eavesdrop"[26] on — what is generally agreed upon among contemporary scientists (biologists, astrophysicists, cosmologists), they will find a creation story that enlightens, confirms, and excitingly expands their own religious stories of what the world is and how we are to live within it; more significantly, the universe story will provide a common hermeneutical framework to link a variety of religious stories. Physicist Brian Swimme puts it this way:

> Though scientific knowledge has put lethal weapons in our hands, it has also provided the earth with the first common story of our origins and development. The scientific enterprise has eventuated in a creation myth that offers humanity deeper realization of our bondedness, our profound communion not only within our species, but throughout the living and nonliving universe.
>
> Precisely because this story of the universe comes to us through our investigations beginning with our eyes and ears and body, we can speak of a transcultural creation story. Members of every continent are involved in discovering and articulating this story. Members of every religious tradition are involved in its telling.[27]

25. Thomas Berry and Brian Swimme, *The Universe Story* (San Francisco: Harper & Row, 1992).

26. Sallie McFague, *Models of God: Theology for an Ecological, Nuclear Age* (Philadelphia: Fortress Press, 1988), 86.

27. Brian Swimme, "Science: A Partner in Creating the Vision," in *Thomas Berry and the New Cosmology*, ed. Anne Lonergan and Caroline Richards (Mystic, Conn.: Twenty-Third Publications, 1988), 86.

A fundamental tenet of this scientific creation story resonates with an ingredient in most religious creation or origin stories: since all that exists originates from a common source or process, there is a connectedness, a common stuff, permeating all creatures, living and nonliving. Everything that exists shares a common "cosmological lineage."[28] Sallie McFague describes the "primordial flaring forth" which is the parent of us all:

> In broad strokes, the story emerging from the various sciences claims that some fifteen billion years ago the universe began from a big bang, exploding matter, which was infinitely hot and infinitely concentrated outward to create some hundred billion galaxies, including our galaxy, the Milky Way, itself containing billions of stars and housing our sun and its planet.... All things living and all things not living are the products of the same primal explosion and evolutionary history and hence are interrelated in an internal way right from the beginning. We are cousins to the stars, to the rocks and oceans, to all living creatures.[29]

Besides revealing the common origin and heritage of all creatures, the scientific story also displays how all such creatures function — that is, how they have unfolded and continue to unfold: the entire universe is thoroughly *interrelated and organic;* what one is and what one makes of oneself takes place through dependence on others, through relationships and connectedness. "No tribal myth, no matter how wild, ever imagined a more profound relationship connecting all things in an internal way right from the beginning of time. All thinking must begin with this cosmic genetic relatedness."[30] Such interrelatedness makes for a *dynamic* universe — constantly moving, changing, in process. And this means that the universe is radically *open* — creative of ever new novelty, things never seen or imagined before, yet

---

28. Charlene Spretnak, *States of Grace: The Recovery of Meaning in the Postmodern Age* (San Francisco: Harper & Row, 1991), 20.

29. Sallie McFague, "Cosmology and Christianity: Implications of the Common Creation Story for Theology," in *Theology at the End of Modernity: Essays in Honor of Gordon D. Kaufman,* ed. Sheila Greeve Davaney (Philadelphia: Trinity Press International, 1991), 31.

30. Swimme, "Science: A Partner," 87.

things that have their origin from relatedness to what went before. Such is the picture of our world and our universe offered by this new cosmological myth.

It is a myth that can be taken on, I believe, by most of the world's religious traditions; while it does not contradict the basic content of religious myths of origin, it can clarify, vivify, and perhaps transform them. As with all myth, this cosmological story will give expression to religious convictions and experiences that are already present and at the same time it will give birth to deeper persuasions and a deeper sense of the Creative Source. Perhaps with Berry and Swimme, we can even use a term that theologians have bandied about for centuries: universal revelation. The earth itself, as it is seen by science, can become (I am not saying must become) a source of new insights and feelings for the relation between the Transcendent and the finite. "Our new sense of the universe is itself a type of revelatory experience. Presently we are moving behind any religious expression so far known to the human into a meta-religious age, that seems to be a new comprehensive context for all religions."[31] Given our new awareness of the universe and our sense of ecological kinship with it, we can perhaps speak of the universe as a larger religious community in which the particular and diverse religious communities of history can now recognize each other and come to see how their individual stories are part of the universe story. "Religion begins to appreciate that the primary sacred community is the universe itself. In a more immediate perspective, the sacred community is the Earth community. The human community becomes sacred through its participation in the larger planetary community."[32] Within this newly discovered Earth community, religions can understand themselves and other religions in new ways.

Such words are visionary; they do not represent what is presently going on in the world of religions. But given the truth of what we know about the universe, given our momentous responsibilities to it, is it not a vision worthy of our trust and

---

31. Berry and Swimme, *The Universe Story,* 255.
32. Ibid., 257.

commitment? Is it not a vision that will help remedy the insularity and antagonism that has darkened and twisted so much of our religious histories?

> This common story is available to be remythologized by any and every religious tradition and hence is a place of meeting for the religions, whose conflicts in the past and present have often been the cause of immense suffering and bloodshed as belief is pitted against belief. What this common story suggests is that our primary loyalty should be not to nation or religion but to the earth and its Creator (albeit that Creator may be understood in different ways).[33]

A common ethical story: What we know about the earth and the universe today provides religions not only with the possibility of a shared religious story but also, and I think more important, with the necessity of a common ethical task and the shared guidelines to carry out that task. Again, it is especially on the ethical level that the universe story can exercise a practical unifying force among the religions; at the same time, the task with which our common creation story challenges us can provide a compelling response to the relativizing corrosion of a postmodern attitude which insists that any attempt at common ethical programs or criteria is destined to drown in the sea of diversity.

The chapter in the universe story that is currently being lived out and written might fittingly be titled, in the words of Harvard biologist Edward O. Wilson: "Is Humanity Suicidal?"[34] We are indeed "flirting with the extinction of our species" (ibid.) as we witness and cause the extinction of thousands of other species. The task of preventing this suicide, and the broader geocide, is the most compelling and unsettling ethical imperative facing humankind today. "In spite of continuing political tensions among nations, the most dangerous threat to the world's well-being is not war but the closing down of the earth's most basic systems, which support us and all other forms of life."[35] Not to

---

33. McFague, "Cosmology and Christianity," 34.
34. Edward O. Wilson, "Is Humanity Suicidal?" *New York Times Magazine,* May 30, 1992, 24–29.
35. McFague, "Cosmology and Christianity," 20.

respond to this threat and this ethical imperative is to renounce or diminish one's humanity. Because this is true for peoples in all cultures, of all religions (in different degrees, of course, for the impoverished campesino than for the multinational executive), our common universe story, with its ecological awareness and demands, provides us with the motivation and the means to break the roadblock that many people try to place before any kind of universal ethical venture based on universal ethical criteria. To the postmodern insistence that every value or every moral project is but an individual social construction valid only for its own backyard, to the refusal of many today to endorse any kind of universal or "meta" discourse that would rally the troops in a united campaign, we can hold up our common universe story that tells us we are all interrelated in our origins, in our functioning, *and* in our responsibility for saving our species and endangered planet. With Charlene Spretnak, I think we can speak of "the 'metadiscourse' of the universe" which can link our individual discourses, or of the "grand cosmologic" that can inform the logic of all cultures. Before we are located in our separate, diverse cultural-religious houses, we are located, more deeply, decisively, and responsibly, in the cosmic neighborhood, in the one world in which we all share and which connects us all with each other and which, today, pleads with us for its own salvation.[36]

There is, therefore, a "place" where we all stand together, where we share both common experiences, concerns, and responsibilities: our earth — beautiful in its mysterious connectedness and evolution but also menaced in the devastation that the human species has wrought upon it. This earth provides the religions not only with a religious community in which they can share myths of origin, but also with an ethical community in which they can identify and defend common criteria of truth. In their basic content, such criteria will probably be something like those being worked out by international ecological groups, especially nongovernmental criteria that seek to balance the promotion of life for individuals and for ecosystems. I'm not claiming that such universal ethical criteria are ready-made

---

36. Spretnak, *States of Grace*, 81, 105.

or that they can be neatly articulated in a kind of ecological Decalogue. But I am stating that the universe story, or the new creation myth, which religions can today communally affirm will provide them with the materials and perspectives with which to successfully, though never finally, work out global ecological norms.[37]

The religions of the world have a special, perhaps determinative, role in responding to the ethical-ecological demands of our common creation myth. Many people engaged in the environmental struggle are coming to realize the truth contained in the reminder of Native American and other primal spiritualities that to save our earth from impending ecological devastation more is needed than practical programs and new political-economic policies; as essential as such practical, concrete measures surely are, they will turn out to be ineffective or unpersuasive for both individuals and nations unless they are nurtured and animated by a sense of the sacredness of the earth. If we regard the earth and all its creatures as merely finite, as disposable tools to achieve our own good, we will not dispel our ecological nightmares; what we need, in Christian terms, is a truly sacramental awareness of the earth which will enable us to feel the earth as the presence or manifestation or life of the Sacred; the plants and the animals, therefore, have a dignity and value of their own as "children of God" and members, with us, of the divine family. Whether it is expressed is theistic terms (as I just did) or in secular language, some such sense of the sacred or mysterious value of the earth is a prerequisite for an effective ecological program.[38] If the struggle for social justice demands a bedrock of spirituality, this is, perhaps, even more true of the struggle for social justice and the integrity of creation.

---

37. One set of such general norms was suggested by the International Coordinating Committee on Religion and the Earth for the Earth Summit in Rio de Janeiro. The committee formulated a statement of "Ethics for Living" which called on all people to live sustainably (with a concern for the present *and* for the future), justly, frugally, peacefully, interdependently, knowledgeably (recognizing the need for ecological education), and holistically (fostering the whole person, spiritually, physically, intellectually). See "An Earth Charter," mentioned in note 24.

38. Seyyed Hossein Nasr, "Islam and the Environmental Crisis," in *Spirit and Nature: Why the Environment Is a Religious Issue,* ed. Steven C. Rockefeller and John C. Elder (Boston: Beacon Press, 1992), 105–6.

And I would hold that most, if not all, of the world's spiritualities can respond meaningfully to that task. Not always in their actual behavior through history but generally in the original vision and teachings of their founders, the "wisdom traditions" that have successfully made it through the obstacle course of human history all teach some form of respect for life, of interconnectedness, and of the need to overcome self-aggrandizement and to treat others as we would want them to treat us. As initial efforts have already indicated, spokespersons for the world's religious communities are forming a common front in revealing and opposing the self-centeredness, the consumerism, the disregard for life that feed the monster of ecological devastation now consuming the globe. Here especially the religions can unite.[39]

So when our efforts for a globally responsible interreligious dialogue are challenged with the fitting question of "Whose justice are you talking about?," we can give one clear and equally challenging response: the earth's justice! Yes, the critics are right — every understanding of justice is socially mediated and motivated. But here is one form of justice that we must all not only be concerned about but in some way agree on: all nations and religions must devote themselves to the common task of saving and sustaining the integrity and life-giving powers of the planet. If the job is not done jointly, it won't really be done! It is as simple, and yet as profound, as that. So the hope expressed by Thomas Berry is as idealistic as it is imperative, and it seems to me that we have no choice but to endorse it: "Concern for the well-being of the planet is the one concern that hopefully will bring the nations [and the religions] of the world into an inter-nation [and inter-religious] community."[40]

Eco-human Well-Being:
A Universal Criterion for Truth

Having proposed that all religions show the capability of genuine concern for human well-being in this world, then having de-

---

39. Spretnak, *States of Grace*, 9.
40. Thomas Berry, *The Dream of the Earth* (San Francisco: Sierra Club Books, 1988), 218.

scribed how the state of the present world (especially the drama of the universe story) is calling forth this capability, I must recognize the stubborn truth that there is no clear, identifiable unity among the religious communities on how we are to respond to the needs of this suffering planet. The specter of diversity once again rears its defiant head and announces the counterclaim: "Okay, the sufferings of people and planet may present the religions with a common problem. But just because you have a common problem (maybe even a common diagnosis of the problem), you don't have the assurance of a common answer." Thus, the question of "Whose justice?" can never be simply or totally dismissed. The diversity of religious experience and traditions will not allow it.

David Tracy states the problem more academically and more pointedly:

> There are family resemblances among the religions. But as far as I can see, there is no single essence, no one content of enlightenment or revelation, no one way of emancipation or liberation to be found in all that plurality...there are different interpretations of what way we should follow to move from a fatal self-centeredness to a liberating Reality-centeredness.... The responses of the religions, their various narratives, doctrines, symbols, and their often conflicting accounts of the way to authentic liberation are at least as different as they are similar. They are clearly not the same.[41]

Eco-Human Justice: A Cross-Cultural Criterion

How can we fashion consensus out of such stubborn diversity? How can we mediate between two differing views about what will ensure authentic liberation? In a particular context, for instance, a Buddhist calls for the total selflessness of nonviolence, while a Christian urges the self-giving of armed resistance. How might a shared commitment to global responsibility and eco-human justice help adjudicate the truth between them? Can what I am calling *soteria* really function as a common means by which

---

41. Tracy, *Plurality and Ambiguity,* 90, 92.

persons from differing religions can, not only listen to and learn
from each other, but also criticize each other, correct each other,
and so come together to articulate and live truth claims that they
feel are universal?

Tracy himself tries to show how religious diversity does not
necessarily means religious divergence. Genuine conversation, he
believes, can take place between really different, even contrasting,
religious perspectives; religious communities *can* resolve their differences. Tracy outlines three general criteria for religious truth
which he thinks could be acceptable to persons of different religious traditions and which therefore can enable them to reach
joint judgments:

(a) "The truth of a religion is, like the truth of its nearest
cousin, art, primordially the truth of manifestation."[42] In
religion, we know something to be so because it *manifests*
or reveals itself to us; we know it because, like the beauty
of art, we feel it. More practically, it *makes a claim* on us;
it grasps or lays hold of us. So, if the stories or rituals of
your religion can tug at and claim my heart, if I feel their
truth manifested before me at least as a "suggestive possibility,"[43] I can share your truth, and so we can come to mutual
agreement.

(b) But what touches the heart must also listen to the head;
even though there is no cross-cultural consensus on what
"reasonability" means or requires, Tracy believes that all
religions will recognize the need for some kind of "cognitive criteria of coherence with what we otherwise know or,
more likely, believe to be the case."[44] However we work out
the connections, religious truth known primarily through
the heart must be brought into a productive conversation with the intellectual truths we know through common
sense, good thinking, and our scientific understanding of
the world.

---

42. Tracy, *Dialogue*, 43.
43. Ibid., 40.
44. David Tracy, "God, Dialogue, and Solidarity," 901.

(c) Finally, there must also be "ethical-political criteria on the personal and social consequences of our beliefs."[45] How do our religious experience and beliefs make for a better world, both our own and that of society? Tracy offers two reasons why all religions could agree on the validity and necessity of such criteria: "First, the religions themselves — especially but not solely in their prophetic strands — demand this. Secondly, our very nature as human beings demands ethical assessment."[46]

Certainly, all three of Tracy's criteria — the mystical, the reasonable, the ethical — must enter into the mix that is inter-religious dialogue; all three must contribute to the process of making shared assessments of truth. But if we ask which of these criteria can best help us break through the postmodern roadblock of "incommensurability," if we explore which of them offers what religions have most in common, then I urge that the most reliable and applicable criterion is that of ethical-political concern for human and ecological suffering. Here we find common and usable materials to make the first crossings between our differing cultural religious perspectives.

The religious or mystical experience of what Tracy calls manifestation and the determination of the cognitive criteria that make for reasonability are much more subjectively or culturally conditioned than are the ethical demands arising from starvation or destruction of the rain forests (though all ethical responses are to some extent culturally colored). Ethical and liberative criteria, insofar as they are directed toward problems or issues that are truly common to us all, are better able to serve as the starting point or foundation with which we can move on to discuss the manifestation and the rational coherence of our individual truth claims. And if, as I suggested earlier, such common ethical struggles can lead us to *shared manifestations of a Power or Sacred Mystery* that animates our global responsibility, then we have an even more reliable common criterion for truth.

---

45. Ibid.
46. Tracy, *Dialogue*, 46.

So of the three cross-cultural criteria for working toward shared assessments of truth among the incorrigibly diverse world religions — personal experience, cognitive coherence, and ethical fruits — it is the last criterion that is "most cross-cultural." Questions concerning the ethical fruits of a particular belief or practice — that is, whether it does remove suffering and promote well-being — provide common ground on which persons of differing traditions can stand and effectively discuss their differences and work toward consensus. The critical data regarding the ethical effects of one's claims are, as it were, much more "at hand" than are appeals to one's religious experience or to what makes rational sense. One's own religious experience or one's way of being reasonable are buried deeper below the sediment of culture and society; certainly we can dig them out and share them; but I am urging that there is other ground, more accessible and more urgent, on which we can begin our sharing.

If followers of various religious traditions can agree in the beginning that whatever else their experience of truth or of the Divine or of Enlightenment may bring about, it must always promote greater eco-human well-being and remove the sufferings of our world, then they have a shared reference point from which to affirm or criticize each other's claims. Such ethical concerns do not provide immediate solutions to interreligious disagreements, but they do constitute a walkable path toward such solutions.

So I would agree with Francis Schüssler Fiorenza when he proposes "solidarity with the suffering" as the source of criteria that will enable persons from diverse cultures and religions to come to shared conclusions about truth and value and action. Such ethical solidarity affirms the diversity of viewpoints and thus warns against the danger of an "objectivism" of only one absolute perspective; but it also demands that out of the diversity we make judgments and take action that will relieve the suffering; thus it avoids the dangers of postmodern relativism.[47]

Precisely because human and ecological suffering is both *uni-*

---

47. Francis Schüssler Fiorenza, "Theological and Religious Studies: The Contest of the Faculties," in *Shifting Boundaries: Contextual Approaches to the Structure of Theological Education*, ed. Barbara G. Wheeler and Edward Farley (Louisville: Westminster/John Knox, 1991), 133–34.

versal and *immediate* it can serve all religious persons as a common context and criterion for assessing religious truth claims. In its universality, human and ecological suffering confronts and affects us all; in its immediacy, it has a raw reality and challenge that are somehow beyond our differing interpretations of it. This is why "suffering brings us to the bedrock of human existence and cuts through the hermeneutical circle."[48] The stark image of a child starving because of poverty or of a lake polluted because of chemical dumping has an immediacy that breaks through our differing cultural interpretations of it. It stares us in the face and questions us before we can fully understand or interpret it. It is this questioning face of the suffering that enables religions to question each other and come to joint assessments of truth. Thus, a concern for ethical-political criteria when confronted with suffering can work cross-culturally.

But in order to work, it is not enough that the participants in interreligious dialogue simply "bear in mind" the reality of the suffering, of the victims of human or ecological injustice; it is not enough that they all announce to each other and the world that they are "globally responsible." If ethical-political criteria resulting from "solidarity with the suffering" are really to bear fruit in the dialogue, if the "hermeneutical privilege of the oppressed" is really to function as a source of dialogical decision making, then the suffering oppressed themselves and those who can speak for the oppressed species and earth will have to be not simply the *object* of the dialogue, but active *participants* in it. If their voices are to be heard, they will have to be present as they generally have not been within the arena of interreligious dialogue. The suffering, the victims, will have to have an active part in determining the agenda for the dialogue, the procedure and format, yes, the place and the language, too! Just how all this can be arranged is not easy to say, for certainly this has not been the style or the practice of dialogical conferences as they have been planned and practiced over the past decades; the excluded will now have to be included. If religious spokespersons are serious about basing their discussions on ethical-political criteria and on

---

48. Ibid., 135.

global responsibility, then they will have to prove this serious-
ness by inviting to the dialogue those most affected by present
realities.

But what is required is more than simply inviting the suffering and oppressed to the table of dialogue. If their voices are to
be not only heard but understood, if the reality of their suffering
and ethical concerns are to be felt and not just registered, then
somehow all the participants in the dialogue need to be *actively
involved in the praxis* of working against eco-human injustice
and promoting more life-giving, just ethical-political policies in
the structures of governments and economics. One can hear the
message of the suffering only if one is struggling, and therefore suffering, together with them. Dialogical conversation must
include, in some way, dialogical praxis for liberation and well-
being. Just what this means and how it can be carried out will
vary from context to context.

With these other voices representing the suffering of humanity
and of the earth actively present in our interreligious discourse,
participants will be able to apply ethical-political criteria all
the more realistically and effectively. Those speaking for the
marginalized and oppressed can serve, as it were, as "arbiters"
or a "court of appeal" when there are differing views among the
religious spokespersons as to just what are the ethical fruits of
a particular religious claim. Such decisions, in other words, are
not to be made only, or primarily, by the "religious experts." The
persons directly affected will give witness about just how their
lives have been changed and enhanced, or limited and threatened,
by a particular religious conviction or behavior. They will make
known, for instance, how images of God as transcendent or immanent affect their attitudes to this world, how beliefs in karma
or afterlife have contributed to their well-being now, how non-
violent or armed forms of resistance can improve their situation.
Not that their views or experiences will be the final verdict in
any discussion. Still, I am convinced that their voices will generally be an effective, if not decisive, help in the difficult task of
honoring the diversity of religious views and yet formulating out
of that diversity decisions and programs that will promote global
responsibility.

Liberative Dialogue: A Proposal, Not a Program

In holding up global responsibility or concern for eco-human liberation and well-being as the context and criterion for interreligious dialogue, I hope it is clear that I am offering to my religious brothers and sisters a broad proposal, not a neatly defined program. I am offering an approach to the dialogue, not a fixed set of rules or definitions.

It is an approach that is based on something that many people propose as the foundation for all dialogue: conversion.[49] I came calling on all participants in interreligious dialogue to share in a common conversion. But the conversion I mean here is not the explicitly religious conversion of mystical experience or enlightenment (though that is certainly not excluded) but the "worldly" conversion of devoting oneself unrestrictedly to the well-being of our suffering brothers and sisters and planet. If all participants in dialogue are genuinely converted to eco-human well-being, if this is the prereligious priority in their lives, then I am quite certain that something like the globally responsible dialogue outlined here will work.[50]

Just how it will work cannot be known before the dialogue itself. As David Tracy has described every serious conversation, *solvitur ambulando* — loosely: we will know the path by walking it.[51] What our global responsibility and our commitment to eco-human justice mean and require in particular situations can be determined only within those situations — on the basis of unreserved listening to each other, directed by our conversion to the suffering neighbor or planet, inspired by the witness of the victims themselves; as we walk and talk and act together, we will make our decisions. Why the decisions are correct, why we must

---

49. Bernard Lonergan, *Method in Theology* (New York: Herder & Herder, 1972), 101–24, 267–93.

50. The "worldly" conversion I am privileging is not really opposed to the "religious" conversion that Bernard Lonergan speaks about. Indeed, in light of what I said about the world as a context for religious expression, I understand such a conversion to the well-being of the world and others to be a conversion to the Great Mystery. Thus, such a conversion is not really a "prereligious priority"; it is deeply religious, for it is in the experience of loving our neighbor that we discover the Mystery that animates and grounds such "worldly" love.

51. Tracy, *Plurality and Ambiguity*, 47.

sometimes agree with or learn from our fellow participants in dialogue and sometimes oppose them — this will be much more a matter of feeling, of ethical intuition than of hard-and-fast rules. We are talking here of *phronesis* — the ability of the good person to know the good, of the ethically converted to know the ethical.[52]

And as persons of different religious communities walk this path of a globally responsible dialogue, they will discover not only what the suffering world demands of them but also what they have to offer. At the beginning here, I tried to show that all religions have the ability to respond to the ethical demands of our threatened world, that they all have a liberative content in their scriptures and traditions. But this ability or this content may lie hidden, or it may be in the form of seeds needing nurture in order to grow. A conversion to the well-being of others and the earth may be, in other words, the occasion for religions to rediscover themselves and to see, as perhaps they have never seen before, the this-worldly liberative power in their stories and rituals. In his concluding comments on a book that tries to assemble the liberative message of various religions, William Burrows admits the ability of various (all?) religions to respond to the demands of eco-human justice — and to see themselves differently in that response:

> What is indubitable is that our authors [*World Religions and Human Liberation*] show that the liberation praxis motif is capable of being subsumed into various traditions as they ponder responses to the contradictions, injustices, and outrages of the present. . . . That traditions as varied as those represented in this book can envisage the future as

---

52. What George Lindbeck said of the "norms of reasonableness" fits nicely with what I am trying to say of the norms of global responsibility: "the norms of reasonableness are too rich and subtle to be adequately specified in any general theory of reason or knowledge. . . . The norms . . . are like the rules of depth grammar, which linguists search for and may at times approximate but never grasp. The reasonable [or, the globally responsible] in religion and theory, as in other domains, has something of that aesthetic character, that quality of unformalizable skill, which we usually associate with the artist or the linguistically competent." George Lindbeck, *The Nature of Doctrine: Religion and Theology in a Postliberal Age* (Philadelphia: Westminster Press, 1984), 130.

one of resisting oppression in liberationist modes, I suggest, says more about the openness of great traditions to radical reinterpretation and reorientation than it does about liberation as a central motif in their classical constitution. To that extent, liberation can fairly be called a commensurable concept. But it may have to become so *as these traditions address the future more than as retrievals of their past.*[53]

And if this process is carried out — if different religious communities respond to this challenge of interpreting themselves and listening to and learning from others on the common ground of global responsibility — then these communities will also *create* a response to the postmodern criticisms and concerns we mentioned earlier. It will be a response that both affirms and yet goes beyond what our postmodern awareness tells us about the cultural construction and limitations of all truth and ethical positions. Yes, the ultimate foundation for any ethical stance is the community in which it was created and for which it makes sense. But today, given the anguished needs of our species and our earth, all of us are offered both the necessity and possibility of belonging to *both* our particular ethical communities *and* to the global ethical community. Our truth claims and our ethical decisions must be — and *can* be — formed not only in our individual community but also in our global community. Certainly, this global

---

53. William Burrows, "Commensurability and Ambiguity: Liberation as an Inter-religiously Usable Concept," in *World Religions and Human Liberation,* ed. Dan Cohn-Sherbok (Maryknoll, N.Y.: Orbis Books, 1992), 127–42. But I would ask Burrows what makes it possible for the religions to respond to the future as they are doing. It must be something in their past and in their given identity that is retrieved, revisioned, and reaffirmed and then used as their response to the future. Peter Donovan agrees essentially with Burrows when he points out that although we cannot maintain that the different religions have the same answers to the global questions of our times, we do see that they have the ability to respond to the same questions and provide answers that are more compatible than contradictory: "Pronouncements like that of the Dalai Lama ('All religions teach common moral precepts') are not to be taken, then as descriptions of an actual state of affairs. They are, rather, pleas for religions to make common cause (in the interests, in this case, of world peace), interpreting and adjusting their traditions of belief so as to be able intentionally to affirm such common concerns as moral." Peter J. Donovan, "Do Different Religions Share Moral Common Ground?" *Religious Studies* 22 (1986): 375.

community of dialogical ethical discourse is not yet present; but it can be formed, and it is forming.[54]

It will be a "community of communities," a paradoxical but actual community in which we belong both to our own religion and culture and yet genuinely participate in the global community struggling for eco-human justice and well-being. It will be a community in which we are both particularists and universalists, making strong claims on the basis of our particular religious convictions but knowing that such claims might be relativized in the wider conversation with other strong claims and with the even stronger demand to remove human and ecological suffering.

If there are those who say such an ethical community of communities is a pipe dream, then I respond respectfully but firmly that we have no choice today but to dream such dreams.

54. Linnel Cady, "Foundation or Scaffolding: The Possibility of Justification in an Historical Approach to Ethics," *Union Seminary Quarterly Review* 41 (1987): 45–62.

Chapter 7

Two Types of Unity and Religious Pluralism

Masao Abe and Donald W. Mitchell

In the contemporary world of religious pluralism not only the mutual understanding between world religions, but also the mutual transformation between them through dialogue is necessary because we now exist in a world in which many people question the legitimacy of not only a particular religion such as Christianity, Buddhism, or Islam, but also the legitimacy of religion as such. The most crucial task of any religion in our time is, beyond mutual understanding, to elucidate the raison d'être of religion as such. In the following I would like to suggest how mutual transformation is possible by discussing three issues: first, a monotheistic God and the realization of *Nichts* (Nothingness); second, two types of unity or oneness; and third, justice and wisdom.

A Monotheistic God and the Realization of Nichts (Nothingness)

Western scholars often discuss religion in terms of a contrast between ethical religion and natural religion (C. P. Tile), prophetic religion and mystical religion (F. Heiler), and monotheistic religion and pantheistic religion (W. F. Albright, A. Lang), with the first in each pair referring to Judeo-Christian-Muslim religions and the second to most of the Oriental religions. This kind of bifurcation has been set forth by Western scholars with such "Western" religions as Judaism, Christianity, and Islam as the standard of comparative judgment. Consequently, non-Semitic

Oriental religions are often not only lumped together under a single category, despite their rich variety, but also grasped from outside without any penetration into their inner religious core. Unlike the Semitic religions, which most Western scholars recognize as having a clear common character, such Oriental religions as Hinduism, Buddhism, Confucianism, Taoism, and Shinto exhibit significant differences in their religious essences, and hence, cannot legitimately be classified into a single category. Partly in order to bring this point into sharper focus, and partly because I am here to represent Buddhism I will take up Buddhism alone from among the Oriental religions and contrast it with Judaism, Christianity, and Islam.

Most Western scholars correctly characterize Judaism, Christianity, and Islam *not* as natural, mystical, and pantheistic religions, but as ethical, prophetic, and monotheistic religions. All three religions are based on the One Absolute God: Yahweh in Judaism, God the Father in Christianity, and Allah in Islam. In each of these religions the One God is believed to be a personal God who is essentially transcendent to human beings, but whose will is revealed to human beings through prophets and who commands people to observe certain ethicoreligious principles. Although we should not overlook some conspicuous differences in emphasis among these three religions, we can say with some justification that they are ethical, prophetic, and monotheistic.

In contrast, Buddhism does not talk about One Absolute God who is essentially transcendent to human beings. Instead, it teaches *pratītya-samutpāda,* that is the law of "dependent coordination" or "conditional co-production" as the Dharma, Truth. This teaching emphasizes that everything in and beyond the universe is interdependent, co-arising, and co-ceasing (not only temporally, but also ontologically) with everything else. Nothing exists independently, or can be said to be self-existing. Accordingly, in Buddhism everything without exception is relative, relational, nonsubstantial, and changeable. Even the divine (Buddha) does not exist by itself, but is entirely interrelated to humans and nature. This is why Gautama Buddha, the founder of Buddhism, did not accept the age-old Vedantic notion of Brahman, which is believed to be the sole and enduring reality underlying the universe. For a similar reason, Buddhism cannot accept the monotheistic notion of One Absolute God as the ultimate reality, but advocates *śūnyatā* (emptiness) and *tathatā* (suchness or as-it-is-ness) as the ultimate reality.

Śūnyatā as the ultimate reality in Buddhism literally means "emptiness" or "voidness" and can imply "absolute nothingness." This is because *śūnyatā* is entirely unobjectifiable, unconceptualizable, and unattainable by reason and will. It also indicates the absence of enduring self-being or the nonsubstantiality of everything in the universe. It is beyond all dualities and yet includes them.

In the realization of *śūnyatā*, not only sentient beings but also the Buddha, not only *saṁsāra*, but also *nirvāṇa* are without substance and are empty. Accordingly, neither Buddha nor *nirvāṇa*, but the realization of the nonsubstantiality of everything that is, the realization of *śūnyatā* is ultimate.

This realization of the nonsubstantial emptiness of everything is inseparably related with the law of dependent coorigination. Dependent coorigination as the Dharma (truth) is possible only when everything in the universe is without fixed, enduring substance (although possessing relative, temporal substance) and is open in its relationship with everything else. We human beings have a strong disposition to reify or substantialize objects as well as our own self as if they were permanent and unchangeable substances. This substantialization of and the accompanying attachment to objects cause human suffering. The most serious case of this problem lies in the substantialization of the self (which results in self-centeredness) and the substantialization of one's own religion (which entails a religious imperialism). Buddhism emphasizes the awakening to *śūnyatā* (that is, the nonsubstantiality of everything, including self and Buddha) in order to be emancipated from suffering. Thus it teaches nonself (*anātman*) and awakening to Dharma rather than faith in the Buddha.

However, Buddhist emphasis on no-self and emptiness, as Buddhist history has showed, often causes indifference to the problem of good and evil and especially social ethics. Buddhists must learn from monotheistic religion how human personality can be comprehended on the basis of the impersonal notion of "Emptiness," and how to incorporate I-Thou relationships into the Buddhist context of Emptiness.

In Christianity God is not simply transcendent. Rather, God is deeply immanent in humankind as the incarnation of the Logos in human form, namely, Jesus Christ. And yet the divine and the human are not completely interdependent. For while the human definitely is dependent upon God, God is not dependent upon the human. The world cannot exist without God, but God can exist without the world. This is because God is the self-existing deity. God can and does exist by himself without depending on anything else. In this regard, Buddhists may ask, "What is the ground of one God who is self-existence?" The Christian might answer this question by stressing the importance of faith in God, this faith being nothing but the "assurance of things hoped for, the conviction of things not seen" (Heb. 11:1). Further, God in Semitic religion is not merely the One Absolute God in the ontological sense, but a living and personal God who calls humans through his word and humans must respond to his word.

In his book, *Does God Exist?*, Hans Küng says, "God in the bible is subject and not predicate: it is not that love is God, but that God is love — God is one who faces me, whom I can address" (64).

My Buddhist reaction to this statement is as follows: Can I not address God, not from the outside of God, but from within God? Again, is it not that God faces me within God even if I turn my back on God? The God who faces me and whom I address is God as subject. However, the God within whom I address God and within whom God meets me is not God as subject, but rather God as predicate. Or, more strictly speaking, that God is neither God as subject nor God as predicate, but God as *Nichts*. In God as *Nichts,* God as subject meets me even if I turn my back on that God and I can truly address that God as Thou. The very I-Thou relationship between the self and God takes place precisely in God as *Nichts*. Since God as *Nichts* is the *Ungrund* ground of the I-Thou relationship between the self and God, God as *Nichts* is neither subject nor predicate, but a copula that acts as a connecting, intermediating link between the subject and the predicate. This entails that God as *Nichts* is *Nichts* as God: God is *Nichts* and *Nichts* is God. And on this basis we may say that God is love and love is God because *Nichts* is the unconditional, self-negating love. This is the absolute interior of God's mystery which is its absolute exterior at one and the same time. We may thus say:

> God is love because God is *Nichts*.
> *Nichts* is God because *Nichts* is love.

This interpretation may not accord with traditional orthodoxy. Here, however, both human longing for salvation and the deepest mystery of God are thoroughly fulfilled. Further, God as subject who meets one and whom one can address as Thou is incompatible with the autonomous reason so important to modern humanity, and so also nowadays challenged by Nietzschean nihilism and atheistic existentialism. The notion of God as *Nichts*, however, is not only compatible with but also can embrace autonomous reason because there is no conflict between the notion of God as *Nichts* (which is neither subject nor predicate) and autonomous reason, and because the autonomy of rational thinking, however much it may be emphasized, is not limited by the notion of God as *Nichts*. In the self-negating or self-emptying God who is *Nichts*, not only are modern human autonomous reason and rationalistic subjectivity overcome without being marred, but also the mystery of God is most profoundly perceived. God as love is fully and most radically grasped far beyond contemporary atheism and nihilism.

This is my humble suggestion to the understanding of God today.

Two Types of Unity or Oneness

To any religion, the realization of the oneness of ultimate reality is important because religion is expected to offer an integral and total — rather than fragmental or partial — salvation from human suffering. Even a so-called polytheistic religion does not believe in various deities without order, but it often worships a certain supreme deity as a ruler over a hierarchy of innumerable gods. Further, the three major deities often constitute a trinity — as exemplified by the Hindu notion of *Trimūrti,* the threefold deity of Brahmā, Vishṇu, and Śiva. Such a notion of trinity in polytheism also implies a tendency toward a unity of diversity — a tendency toward oneness.

This means that in any religion, especially in higher religions, the realization of the Oneness of ultimate reality is crucial. Yet, the realization of Oneness necessarily entails exclusiveness, intolerance, and religious imperialism, which cause conflict and schism within a given religion and among the various religions. This is a very serious dilemma which no higher religion can escape. How can we believe in the Oneness of the ultimate reality in our own religion without falling into exclusive intolerance and religious imperialism toward other faiths? What kind of Oneness of ultimate reality can solve that dilemma and open up a dimension in which positive tolerance and peaceful coexistence are possible among religions, each of which is based on One Absolute reality?

In this connection I would like to distinguish two kinds of oneness or unity: first, monotheistic oneness or unity; second, nondualistic unity or oneness. It is my contention that not the former but the latter kind of unity or oneness may provide a real common basis for the contemporary pluralistic situation of world religions. How, then, are monotheistic and nondualistic oneness different from one another? I would like to clarify their differences by making the following four points.

First, monotheistic oneness is realized by distinguishing itself and setting itself apart from dualistic twoness and pluralistic manyness. Monotheism essentially excludes any form of dualism and pluralism and, therefore, stands in opposition to them. Precisely because of this oppositional relation, monotheistic oneness is neither a singular oneness nor a truly ultimate Oneness. In order to realize true Oneness we must go not only beyond dualism and pluralism, but also beyond monotheistic oneness itself. Then we can realize nondualistic oneness, because at that point we are completely free from any form of duality, including the duality between monotheism and dualism or pluralism.

Second, in monotheism God is the ruler of the universe and the lawgiver to humans, and his being is only remotely similar and comparable to beings of the world. Although the monotheistic God is accessible by prayer and comes to be present among humans through love and mercy, his transcendent character is undeniable. The monotheistic God is somewhat "over there," not completely right here and right now. Contrary to this case, nondualistic oneness is the ground or root source realized right here and right now, from which our life and activities can properly begin. When we overcome monotheistic oneness we come to a point which is neither one nor two, nor many, but which is appropriately referred to as "zero" or "nonsubstantial emptiness." Since the "zero" is free from any form of duality and plurality, true oneness can be realized through the realization of "zero." My use of "zero" in this regard, however, may be misleading, because the term is used to indicate something negative. But here in this context I use "zero" to indicate the principle which is positive and creative as the source from which one, two, many, and the whole can emerge. Since I use "zero" not in a negative sense but positive and creative sense I may call it "great zero." Monotheistic oneness is a kind of oneness which lacks the realization of "great zero," whereas nondualistic oneness is a kind of oneness which is based on the realization of "great zero."

Third, the true oneness which can be attained through the realization of "great zero" should not be objectively conceived. If it is objectified or conceptualized in any way, it is not real oneness. An objectified oneness is merely something named "oneness." To reach and fully realize true oneness, it is necessary to completely overcome conceptualization and objectification. True oneness is realized only in a nonobjective way by overcoming even "great zero" objectified as an end or goal. Accordingly, overcoming "great zero" as an end is a turning point from the objective, aim-seeking approach to the nonobjective, immediate approach, from monotheistic oneness to nondualistic oneness. Monotheistic oneness is oneness before the realization of "great zero," whereas nondualistic oneness is oneness through and beyond the realization of "great zero."

Fourth, monotheistic oneness, being somewhat "over there," does not immediately include two, many, and the whole. Even though it can be all-inclusive, it is more or less separate from the particularity and multiplicity of actual entities-in-the-world. This is because the monotheistic God is a personal God who commands and directs people. Nondualistic oneness, however, which is based on the realization of "great zero" includes all individual things just as they are, without any modification. This is because in nondualistic oneness, conceptualization and objectification are completely and radically overcome. There is no separation between nondualistic oneness and individual things. At this point the one and the many are nondual.

The view of monotheistic unity does not *fully* admit the distinctiveness of uniqueness of each religion united therein, due to the lack of the realization of "great zero" or nonsubstantial emptiness. By contrast, the view of nondualistic unity thoroughly allows the distinctiveness or uniqueness of each religion without any limitation — through the realization of "great zero" or emptiness. This is because the nondualistic unity is completely free from conceptualization and objectification and is without substance. In this nondualistic unity, all world religions with their uniqueness are dynamically united without being reduced to a single principle. This is, however, not an uncritical acceptance of the given pluralistic situation of religions. Instead, the nondualistic unity makes a critical acceptance and creative reconstruction of world religions possible because each religion is grasped in the nondualistic unity — not from the outside but deeply from within in the dynamic laws of a positionless position (i.e., a position which is completely free from any particular position as absolute).

Let me give an example of how world religions can be regrasped from the standpoint of nondualistic unity in a manner that fosters world peace. When the divine, God or Buddha, is believed to be self-affirmative, self-existing, enduring, and substantial, the divine becomes authoritative, commanding, and intolerant. By contrast, when the divine, God or Buddha, is believed to be self-negating, relational, and nonsubstantial, the divine becomes compassionate, all-loving, and tolerant.

If monotheistic religions such as Judaism, Christianity, and Islam place more emphasis on the self-negating, nonsubstantial aspect of their God rather than the self-affirmative authoritative aspect of God — that is, if these religions understand the oneness of absolute God in terms of nondualistic oneness rather than in terms of monotheistic oneness—then they may overcome serious conflicts with other faiths and may establish a stronger interfaith cooperation to contribute to world peace.

Justice and Wisdom

In the Western religions, God is believed to have the attribute of justice, or righteousness as the judge, as well as love or mercy as the forgiver. God is the fountain of justice, so everything God does may be relied upon as just. Since God's verdict is absolutely just, human righteousness may be defined in terms of God's judgment.

The notion of justice or righteousness is a double-edged sword. On the one hand it aids in keeping everything in the right order, but on the other hand it establishes clear-cut distinctions between the righteous and the unrighteous, promising the former eternal bliss, but condemning the latter to eternal punishment. Accordingly, if justice or righteousness is the sole principle of judgment or is too strongly emphasized, it creates serious disunion and schism among people. This disunion is irreparable because it is a result of divine judgment.

Although his religious background was Jewish, Jesus went beyond such a strong emphasis on divine justice and preached the indifference of God's love. Speaking of God the Father, he said, "He makes his sun rise on the evil and on the good, and sends rain on the just and on the unjust" (Matt. 5:45). Thus, he emphasized, "Love your enemies and pray for those who persecute you, so that you may be sons of your Father who is in heaven" (Matt. 5:44–45). Nevertheless, in the Judeo-Christian tradition the notion of divine election is persistently evident. The Old Testament preaches God's choice of Israel from among all the nations of the earth to be God's people in the possession of a covenant of privilege and blessing (Deut. 4:37, 7:6: 1 Kings 3:8: Isa. 44:1–2). In the New Testament, divine election is a gracious and merciful election. Nevertheless, this election is rather restricted, for as the New Testament clearly states, "Many are called, but few are chosen" (Matt. 22:14). Thus, "the terms [election or elect] always imply differentiation whether viewed on God's part or as a privilege on the part of men" (*Baker's Dictionary of Theology,* ed.

Everett F. Harrison, 1960, p. 179). In Christianity the notion of the "Elect of God" often overshadows the "indifference of God's love." If I am not mistaken, this is largely related to the emphasis on justice or righteousness.

While Christianity speaks much about love, Buddhism stresses compassion. Compassion is a Buddhist equivalent to the Christian notion of love. In Christianity, however, love is accompanied by justice. Love without justice is not regarded as true love, and justice without love is not true justice. In Buddhism, compassion always goes with wisdom. Compassion without wisdom is not understood to be true compassion and wisdom without compassion is not true wisdom. Like the Christian notion of justice, the Buddhist notion of wisdom indicates clarification of the distinction or differentiation of things in the universe. Unlike the Christian notion of justice, however, the Buddhist notion of wisdom does not entail judgment or election. Buddhist wisdom implies the affirmation or recognition of everything and everyone in their distinctiveness or in their suchness. Further, as noted above, the notion of justice creates an irreparable split between the just and the unjust, the righteous and the unrighteous, whereas the notion of wisdom evokes the sense of equality and solidarity. Again, justice, when carried to its final conclusion, often results in punishment, conflict, revenge, and even war, whereas wisdom entails rapprochement, conciliation, harmony, and peace. Love and justice are like water and fire: although both are necessary, they go together with difficulty. Compassion and wisdom are like heat and light: although different, they work together complementarily.

The Judeo-Christian tradition, however, does not lack the notion of wisdom. In the Hebrew Bible, wisdom literature such as Job, Proverbs, and Ecclesiastes occupy an important portion in which *hokma* (wisdom) frequently appears. This term refers to both human knowledge and divine wisdom. In the latter case, as a wisdom given by God it enables the human person to lead a good, true, and satisfying life through keeping God's commandments. In the New Testament, *sophia* is understood to be an attribute of God (Luke 11:49), the revelation of the divine will to people (1 Cor. 2:4–7). But most remarkably, Jesus as the Christ is identified with the wisdom of God because he is believed to be the ultimate source of all Christian wisdom (1 Cor. 1:30). Nevertheless, in the Judeo-Christian tradition as a whole, the wisdom aspect of God has been neglected in favor of the justice aspect of God. Is it not important and terribly necessary now to emphasize the wisdom aspect of God rather than the justice aspect of God in order to solve the conflict within religions as well as among religions?

On the other hand, in Buddhism the notion of justice or righteousness is rather weak and thus it often becomes indifferent to social evil and injustice. If Buddhism learns from Western religions the importance of justice, and develops its notion of compassion to be linked not only with wisdom but also with justice, it will become closer to Judaism, Christianity, and Islam in its interfaith relationship and may become more active in establishing world peace.

Unity and Ultimate Reality: A Response to Masao Abe

Masao Abe has presented a very insightful and challenging comparison of two types of unity based on two different ways of understanding ultimate reality. For the Buddhist, true unity must be nondual, free from any duality, and therefore free from any transcendent reality which is not "completely right here and right now." This nondual unity is a social expression of the realization of ultimate reality as emptiness (*śūnyatā* or "great zero"), which includes all things just as they are. The living out of this realization of emptiness entails both wisdom and compassion. Wisdom affirms everything and everyone in their distinctiveness. Compassion cares for everything and everyone within the universal embrace of emptiness in a manner that leads to "rapprochement, conciliation, harmony, and peace."

On the other hand, Abe feels that for the monotheistic Western religions, the social unity realized by a particular religion often stands apart from, and in opposition to, other religions rather than embracing them. This type of sectarian unity reflects a particular monotheistic notion of ultimate reality that can be found in the West. That is, God can be seen as transcendent or, in Abe's words, "somewhat apart" from humankind and the rest of creation. From that transcendent vantage point, God can be seen as judging persons of other faiths rather than including all of them in his loving care. This particular Western picture of God can color one's living out of a monotheistic unity in a way that stresses keeping apart from and judging persons of other faiths. In its most radical form, one sees others not as brothers and sisters to be embraced in solidarity and unity, but as rightful objects of "punishment, conflict, revenge, and even war."

Now this critique of a Western understanding of unity and ultimate reality does not mean that Abe is blind to Buddhist distortions of a life of unity based on the realization of emptiness. He points out that historically in Buddhist practice there has been an indifference to "social evil and injustice." It is true that Buddhists have interpreted the nirvanic unity of ultimate reality in such a naturalistic way that they failed to recognize and confront the particular samsaric evils that assailed their larger societies. These Buddhists enjoyed a social unity within an isolated monastic setting while ignoring the plight of the rest of humanity. Therefore, Abe says that Buddhism can learn much from the West concerning the importance of justice so as to contribute more actively to the establishment of world peace.

But what about the Western religions? How can we overcome the kinds of distortions that Abe has so carefully outlined for us? Abe's own suggestion is that we reunderstand ultimate reality in a way that can be the foundation for a more universal social unity, one that embraces all humankind and even the rest of creation. Abe finds a basis for this reunderstanding in the mystical concept of *Nichts*. *Nichts* is the unconditional, self-emptying (kenotic) love that is the absolute interior of the mystery of God. Abe sees this all-embracing reality as being similar to Buddhist emptiness. It is the "groundless ground" or "boundless openness" in which one finds a deep spiritual unity with all other persons and nature as well. Since *Nichts* embraces everyone and everything, indeed is the very ground of all things, it is not apart from all persons. It can be, therefore, the basis of a nondual social unity that excludes no one, but includes all persons just as they are right here

and now. *Nichts* as ultimate reality cannot be the basis of a social unity of one people of faith against peoples of other faiths.
Rather it provides a theological basis for a social unity that can
foster true and universal harmony and peace between peoples of
different religions, races, and cultures.

As a Christian, I am both attracted to these ideas of Masao
Abe's and a bit cautious at the same time. Let me explain. I am
attracted because I too feel that our understanding of unity is tied
to our understanding of ultimate reality. And, I also agree with
Abe's view that the unity we need today in our pluralistic world
must be one that helps create a new and more united humankind. It cannot be a limited sectarian unity that actually creates
schism and confrontation between peoples, races, cultures, and
religions — that pits the unity of one group over against the unity
of another. So, it is important to understand God from a monotheistic point of view in a way that fosters a more universal unity
of humankind.

My sense of caution arises when Abe suggests that Christians
do this by rediscovering the mystical notion of God as *Nichts*.
This move is typical of modern Zen thinkers, especially of Abe's
Zen colleagues in the Kyoto School. In Zen, true social unity is
the collective self-realization, or self-determination, of the unity
of ultimate reality itself. This means that social unity must be the
communal realization of the interrelated, interpenetrating, nondual unity of emptiness itself. Abe finds something similar to
this nondual understanding of the unity of ultimate reality in the
Western mystical notion of *Nichts* and suggests that Christians
find in it a basis for social unity. Of course it is not that easy.
For example, there are important questions of Christology and
ecclesiology to be addressed.

But these issues aside, what most concerns me is the question of the transcendent personhood of God that Abe seems to
call into question with his Buddhist nondual logic. In this logic,
emptiness is so identified with the forms of life that it cannot be
conceived as existing apart from the world. As I said above, Abe
sees ultimate reality as free from any duality so that it is "completely right here and right now." If we look at *Nichts* through
this Buddhist lens, it is hard to see how the transcendent person-

hood of God can be preserved in the total *kenosis* of *Nichts* so understood. Therefore, I prefer to use a trinitarian logic in understanding *Nichts*. In this logic, *Nichts* is the dynamic love and unity (*perichoresis*) of the Trinity in which each person is defined in relation to the others (the Father is Father only in relation to the Son, etc.) In this way, the transcendent personhood of the Trinity is eternally realized and preserved in the inner-trinitarian life in a manner that would be impossible in a Buddhist-like nondual relation with creation.

It is this preservation of the eternal life of the Trinity that I do not wish to see emptied out in any nondual understanding of the *kenosis* of *Nichts*. On the other hand, I do wish to affirm the kind of universal social unity Abe suggests. I feel that it is possible to ground such a social unity on the trinitarian vision of ultimate reality suggested above. That is, the Christian notion of the Trinity affirms a principle of diversity in unity in a manner that supports the universal unity of humankind. Since God's nature is reflected in his action, the diversity in unity of God's trinitarian nature is also a principle of God's creative action. All humankind is therefore created in a communal image of the diversity in unity of the Trinity. The social realization of this communal image of diversity in unity is the goal of all humankind whereby it realizes its true collective nature.

I have explored the similarities and differences between this Christian trinitarian view and the Buddhist nondual view of a united humankind at some length elsewhere, so I will not repeat myself here.[1] Given the short time I have left, let me just say that I very much appreciate Abe's Buddhist vision of all humankind as "a single, living, self-aware entity."[2] For Abe, to awaken to this fact of our collective existence "in the boundless expanse of Self-awakening" would be the basis of "a united, cooperative, human community in the complete sense of the term."[3] While I interpret

---

1. Donald W. Mitchell, *Spirituality and Emptiness: The Dynamics of Spiritual Life in Buddhism and Christianity* (New York: Paulist Press, 1991). See especially chap. 6.
2. Masao Abe, *Zen and Western Thought* (Honolulu: University of Hawaii Press, 1987), 253.
3. Ibid.

this collective unity of human kind with a trinitarian logic, I share Abe's ideal of living this communal reality for the realization of a greater "communion" of peoples. In this way, all humankind can be full sharers in a more just, peaceful, and united pluralistic world community. For me as a Christian, it is through the communal realization of this true collective nature of humankind that we can achieve the Kingdom of God.

I would like to conclude by saying that both Abe and I agree that we need to replace the modern individualistic vision of independent human persons with a postmodern communalistic vision of a collective humankind in order to realize the type of unity the world so badly needs today. To accomplish this task, we need to examine how our notions of ultimate reality support, or do not support, this new vision that is needed for a more united world community. Do our understandings of ultimate reality enable us to envision an ideal of unity that embraces in kenotic love and compassion all humankind as brothers and sisters? Masao Abe's wonderful presentation — so full of clarity and wisdom — should inspire all of us here to go beyond any sectarian boundaries in order to join together more confidently to work for the ideal that "all may be one" (John 17:21) in a more united, just, and peaceful world.

Chapter 8

Religion, Globality, and Universality

Seyyed Hossein Nasr

The original title assigned to me was "Religion and Globality." I want to modify it and speak about globality as well as universality, which is not quite the same thing. So my comments will embrace not only religion and globality but also universality.

The first question to ask is, why is it that, against the grain of human experience, human history, and our own psychological and mental makeup, we even have to take cognizance of more than one religion? In other words, why is religious pluralism significant? It is not simply because communication on the inner plane has increased. I do not believe that to be the case. The fact that I can watch CNN all over the world does not really mean that communication in depth has increased. There are many examples to the contrary. I know of cases from the civilization from which I come, that is, Islam, of someone writing a letter of invitation to compose a book seven centuries ago in Tabriz and someone responding to it from Tangiers in less than a year, the reply in the form of the written manuscript (which we would never be able to do in the present times). It is not a question of modern communication alone. It is a question of living space, the *Lebensraum* of a part of humanity beginning to lose its homogeneity. I mean that the modern world has been impinging upon the space of the West's homogeneous religious and spiritual life for some time. This attack against the totality of the Western Christian tradition, from the end of the Middle Ages, gradually destroyed the harmony which existed naturally between that particular religion and the living space of those who followed it, leaving a certain empty space. This void gradually began to be felt in the nineteenth century in the West during the very peak of the West's political hegemony over the earth, at the very height of the power of the European empires. In Germany and England and later on in France and other European countries, people began to become interested in Taoism, in the Vedanta, in the Upanishads, in Buddhism, in Islam, and the like, and this phenomenon has continued and in fact intensified to our own day. Moreover, recently, the partial emptying of the space, you might say, of the presence of the Christian tradition within the life of the European West, with increasing modernization, has spilled over from Europe and America to certain other parts of the world. In any case, the partial destruction of the Christian tradition in the West has produced three results: one, the eclipse of religion; two, the appearance of other religions because nature abhors a vacuum, religiously as well as physically; and three, the invention of new religions. All three are actually the results of the events that began to unfold from the middle of the nineteenth century in the West and that have reached a crescendo in our own times.

It is with this background in view that we must understand why pluralism in the field of religion is now itself a crucial religious question. Why is it that most intelligent students on an American campus, if they are serious about their religious interest, cannot be introduced to other religions without taking these religions seriously in the religious sense, whereas a person could have been personally serious in his religious interest, being a devout Catholic or Jew, living in Cordoba with Muslims for eight hundred years without taking a theological interest in Islam? The answer is that it is the inner mental space which has changed, and therefore the question of pluralism has now become a religious question of the utmost importance. In fact, religious people who have been deeply affected by the withering denial of religion by various forms of secularism in the modern world (and here I am not talking of political secularism but philosophical secularism and even secularism within religion) cannot but take the question of pluralism seriously. Therefore the issue continues to come up, and the first question it raises for those who are inter-

ested in religion is the following: Why did God create more than
one religion? Why do we see more than one religion? This is a
very important metaphysical and theological question, and I wish
to answer it by citing a quotation from a very auspicious and also
critical moment in the history of the present cosmic cycle, that is,
the end of the age of prophecy when the last plenary divine message was delivered to humanity, namely, the end of the prophetic
life of the Prophet of Islam. History is proof that after Islam no
new major world religion has appeared upon the scene as such
religions did before. Therefore the moment was extremely important from the point of view of what would follow afterward. I
want to quote a verse from a *surah* of the Quran, as translated
by Martin Lings, a verse which is known to all the Muslims in
the audience but perhaps not to others:

> For each of you we have appointed a law and a way.
> And if God had willed He would have made you one
>   people.
> But He has willed it otherwise that He may put you to the
>   test in what He has given you.
> So vie with one another in good works. Unto God will ye
>   be brought back,
> And He will inform you about that wherein ye differed.
>
> (Quran-V; 51)

That is to say, God will finally inform us on the Day of Judgment as to what were the reasons for the differences among his
religions. In the Islamic tradition this function of revealing what
the differences as well as the inner meaning of these religions are
and the whys of these differences is associated with the function
of the Mahdī, with the spiritual function of this eschatological
figure who will come shortly before the end of this world. But
this function cannot also not be manifested in some way in our
own times.

In any case the fact that these differences exist is, according to
the verse of the Quran, laid down by God and is therefore not
accidental. It is not based on what many people think are local
dogmas. The question is much more profound than that. That
is why one of the great tragedies in the study of religion in the

West and to some extent elsewhere during the last century, both academically and personally in many circles, has been that those who have taken pluralism seriously have been for the most part the very people who have chosen to denigrate divine institutions in the name of human understanding and human accord. This has been the undoing of the raison d'être of religion as sent by God to us in different forms in various parts of the world.

I want to emphasize how difficult is the task of taking religious pluralism seriously. Let me allude to two facts which would appear to be very simple and plain, but which are really important and yet more or less left aside in many of the discourses being carried out, including at this Parliament, and have been often neglected during the intervening one hundred years since this Parliament first met in 1893. And this is true of America and Europe and to a lesser extent of India and other places in the world as well. First of all, each religion has a claim to absoluteness — what the preeminent authority on perennial philosophy, Frithjof Schuon, has called the sense of the Absolute in religions. No one would follow a religion unless he or she felt that there is something absolute in it. Why should people follow something totally relative and therefore transient, whether they be Muslims, Christians, American Indians, Jews, Hindus, Buddhists, or anything else? One would not follow a religion wholeheartedly if one had not sensed that there was something absolute in it. But we do. The second point involves the very simple case of truth; that is, religion makes truth claims.

Of course no Christian will have to be reminded of that fact. Christ said, "Seek the Truth and the Truth shall make you free." Yet, this prominent verse of the Gospel is often put aside when we talk about religions and accord between them. We are afraid to talk about truth in religion, in the same way that we are afraid to talk about truth in any other modern context. It has become an embarrassing term. We never talk about truth at universities these days except in the field of science. Nobody talks about truth in philosophy, in the social sciences, in the humanities; that category is hardly discussed any more. The motto is to "do your own thing" and follow your own individualistic understanding of things including religion.

Now, these two elements are two very simple but fundamental realities about all authentic religions. There is a sense of absoluteness in each religion, and at the center of each religion there is the matter of the truth. Each religion claims to be true. This alone poses for us a horrendous problem: that of multiple truth claims. There is more than one truth claim since there are religions other than our own which also claim to possess truths apparently different from our own and which also claim absoluteness. It is here that the question of pluralism poses its greatest challenge to us and the question of particularism versus universalism becomes so acute. On the one hand, every religion is a form that is revealed to a particular world. By our very earthly existence we are particularized. It is impossible to "exist" in this world of particular forms and claim to be in the same sense in the world of universality. Anyone who does not believe in this metaphysical truth does not know what universality is in the metaphysical sense according to which universality by definition transcends the world of particular forms. If one is talking seriously, one cannot existentially be a pure universalist or a pure esoterist unless one lives beyond the world of forms and exists already in the inward or universal plane. To exist in this world of multiplicity means to live on a plane of existence in which the universal has manifested itself in particularity or the inward in the outward or the essence in form, a point to which I shall turn in a few moments. From one point of view each religion is rooted in particularity, without which we would not have a sense of identity. But this is something, I am sure, about which we do not even have to argue. There is no religion that has not come with a particular language, with a particular sacred history, with particular laws. And yet we see the claim of religions to universality within that very set of particularities.

Now, there are certain religions which, from the very beginning, never claimed that they were meant for the whole of humanity. They are the autochthonous religions, religions which stay put in one place or are associated with only one ethnic group. They are associated with a sacred site, as, for example, Zoroastrianism, the pre-Islamic religion of my own country (Iran), or Hinduism, associated with the sacred land of India, or

Judaism, associated primarily with an ethnic community. There are other religions which claim for themselves a global spread, of which we have three main living examples in the world today: Islam, Christianity, and Buddhism. Or speaking historically, Buddhism, Christianity, and Islam in that order. But this idea of globality and claim to have a message for the whole of humanity must not be confused with universality, which is something else. Not all religions are global but within every religion there exists an element of universality. It is the particularity of a religion that manifests itself in the fact that it addresses people in Sanskrit or Hebrew or Arabic or Pali, or the fact that it does not use a sacred language at all. It can also express itself through a particular rite, even a sacred dance, or through myths which are never written down, as in the primal religions. Yet, whether it claims globality for its message or not, each religion nevertheless possesses a dimension of universality, and this trait is to be seen at the heart of its teachings whether it claims to possess a message for the whole of humanity or only a particular community.

What do we mean here by universality? As we define it, it does not mean that the followers of that religion see the universal message of their religion as applying to every individual in different contexts. That would be globality rather than universality, although the two are often confused with each other. Universality is, in fact, the characteristic of a reality that is not bound by the conditions of time, space, and materiality. A religious message possesses universality when in its heart it transcends all the particularities of the human condition of a particular collectivity to which it addresses itself and which it leads from the level of the particularity of forms to the universality of the formless. And this is true for those global religions I mentioned as well as for those religions which have not traditionally made a global claim, although in the twentieth century some of their members are now trying to globalize them. It should be remembered in passing that in this very city, two blocks from here, Vivekananda tried to globalize Hinduism for the first time. This was not part of the traditional Hindu perspective. Traditionally one could not become Hindu but had to be born into it. The fact that you began to have Vedantic missionaries after 1893 was a new phenomenon in Hinduism. And some other religions which had hitherto been autochthonous followed suit. But here I am talking about the traditional, classical, sacred forms of these religions.

In any case there is a universal element at the heart of all authentic religions whether they address themselves to a particular collectivity or the whole globe without having ever reached all corners of it. There is no religion that has conquered the whole world, and according to a famous ḥadīth of the Prophet that will happen only when the Mahdī appears at the end of time. It will not happen until after the advent of this eschatological event. But despite these claims or lack thereof, universality involves the transcending of a particular set of human conditions and forms. Therefore, the universal appeal of a religion extends beyond the space-time sequel within which it is revealed or within which it is practiced or within which its original forms were established. Now, what is important to remember here is that despite this universality, it is difficult to be able to accept the truth of other religions while clinging to important truth claims of our own religion. There is a tension between the absoluteness and truth of the religion to which we belong and the claim to universality of other religions whether they claim globality or not. And it is to this issue that I wish to address myself now.

One of the tragedies of the study of religion in the last fifty to sixty years has been — academically and also among the more general circle of people interested in other religions in the West and now more and more in other parts of the globe — that the study of religious plurality in the West began at a time when the metaphysical background necessary for such a study did not exist. People began to speak about religious plurality who did not possess the metaphysical and esoteric knowledge necessary for carrying out such a task. This task itself was not completely new. There were instances of pluralism before modern times although under very different conditions from what we see today, including the presence in days of old of the sapiential dimension and the metaphysical knowledge necessary to cross the borders of formal universes. Various religious traditions did meet earlier on and therefore had to come to some kind of *modus vivendi*, as well as some kind of understanding. Two prime examples of this are to be seen in India and Spain. In India, Islam and Hinduism had to live together for a long time, and before that certain forms of Buddhism and Islam had to coexist in that land. In Spain the three monotheistic religions came together. Now we must pose the question: Who were the people in these two instances who were interested in other religions in depth, not in everyday social discourse where sometimes a wonderful harmony prevailed and sometimes not, depending on what the political and economic situations were. Who were those who showed interest in the theological, metaphysical, and spiritual dimensions of the other religions? The answer is that they were usually people who were interested in and penetrated into the inner dimensions of *their own* religion.

Let me limit myself to a field which I know a little bit better, the field of Islam. If one goes down the list and asks who were the people who carried out discourse with the Kabbalists and Christian mystics in Spain, and also to some extent Sicily, one finds that they were invariably people who belonged to the esoteric, inner dimension of Islam. They were usually the Sufis or other Islamic esotericists. The people who were interested only in the legal and institutional aspects of the religion were not the people who usually carried out these discourses in depth, although many of them had wonderful Christian and Jewish friends on the personal level. The same holds true for the Jewish and Christian sides as we see in the case of the grandson of Maimonides, the famous Jewish theologian who became the personal physician to a famous Muslim king, Ṣalāḥ al-Dīn al-Ayyūbī. This grandson 'Obayadah ibn Abraham ibn Moses Maimonides in fact wrote a treatise which some have called a work of Jewish Sufism. One can learn a lesson from our historical experience and contrast it with the lamentable lack of success of academic religious studies in the modern world in the last fifty to sixty years as far as leading to mutual religious understanding and accord are concerned. It is lamentable in the sense that most often works of comparative religious studies have led to the loss of religious faith among many people who have studied them. Such works have often resulted in the relativization of religion and dilution of faith of those who have turned to them, such as many a freshman studying comparative religion in an academic setting. There are of course great exceptions, as we see in the works of such figures as Louis Massignon, W. C. Smith, and Raimon Panikkar. But usually comparative religion is taught in a completely relativistic manner. In many cases students end up either inventing their own religion or taking drugs in the evening to take the place of the religious faith and practice they have lost. Often it leads to students losing serious interest in religion altogether.

Let us also consider the case of the philosophical aspects of religion where all such philosophies are likewise presented as relativities, as people saying different things which contradict each other. It is in this sense that the situation is lamentable. It is in this context that one can say that the study of religions has produced pitiful results. It is sad indeed that the metaphysical background which is necessary for carrying out this task of studying the multiplicity of religions in depth (as well as with spiritual awareness and realization) has been for the most part lacking in the academic study of religions. Those who have usually addressed the question of pluralism have belonged to one of the following categories: there are those who have said that only their own religion is true and nothing else is true; or those who have said that all religions are false; or those who have said, "Let us simply find the lowest common denominator; you put aside half of that in which you believe and I will put aside half of my beliefs and we can then have a common ground on which we can meet." This of course is the worst kind of blasphemy possible in the eyes of God if our religion has any meaning whatsoever because, ultimately, in such a case we are playing the role of God. We decide what part of religion is true and significant and what is not. Instead of submitting to divine authority, we decide to take the exercise of that authority upon ourselves. These three possibilities, of which we all know many examples, have dominated the scene at a time when, in fact, another perspective concerning the study of religion and the meaning of the particularity of sacred forms from a religious point of view has also existed. This perspective is what is now known as the traditional point of view, or that of perennial philosophy, or the *sophia perennis,* as it has sometimes been called.

It is to this oft neglected perspective that I want to address myself because I hold that perspective myself and believe that it is the only perspective which holds the key for accepting the validity of other religions without denigrating our own or violating its integrity, without belittling or reducing the teachings of other religions but respecting them on the highest level, at the level of their truth claims. It must, however, be added that if we accept *all* claims to religious truth on their external level, we still cannot accept everything no matter who claims it to be true. All-inclusivism finally means all-exclusivism. To be all-inclusive of claims of so many modern so-called religions means to make irrelevant the claim of the truth as such. It is not of course this approach which I have in mind.

One can speak of *religio perennis,* the perennial religion, lying at the heart of all authentic religions, the perennial religion of which the perennial philosophy is the intellectual aspect, as I have already mentioned. A foremost expositor in our times of this traditional and perennial philosophy has been Frithjof Schuon. This philosophy, or rather metaphysics, is based on the fundamental principle that the only point of accord between various sacred forms is precisely the inward esoteric dimension; that is, the forms of a religion are not exhausted by their outward limitations, and there is always an inner reality of which the outward is the external form. The outward exists by virtue of the fact that it has issued from the inward. Using another language, one might say that in religion all forms, authentic forms, descend from the transcendent cum immanent dimension. And they are, in a sense, crystallizations in the world of time and space and materiality in which we live of realities which are beyond these dimensions and, by virtue of that, lead us to that other inner dimension. This is the first absolute premise of this point of view: if we limit religions and their truth claims simply to their externality, we will never be able to reach the inner dimension where alone unity is to be found, the unity which also judges and excludes what has issued from only the human level but claims to be religious truth. It is in this inner reality that Schuon "locates" the transcendent unity of religions, "transcendent" being used on purpose to distinguish this unity from some kind of a substantial, material, formal unity which in fact is impossible, as he has stated so elegantly. Although the lack of unity on the plane of forms seems to be somewhat discouraging at first, it is nevertheless true. That is to say, there can be no religious accord on the human plane. Religious accord can only exist on the divine plane. To quote Schuon, "There is no possibility of religious accord in the human atmosphere but only in the divine stratosphere."

By excluding the human experience from the divine stratosphere, we are condemned, in fact, to have many insoluble conflicts in embarking upon the task of penetrating into other authentic religious universes. By limiting the inner meaning of religion (often as a result of confrontation with modernism, which makes a tradition appear as being more and more impervious to its inner reality and closed up to its own inner dimension), nothing else than conflict or at best diplomatic niceties can be expected when religions face each other. We have seen examples of that reality right before our own eyes during the last few decades — what is often incorrectly called "fundamentalism" is nevertheless a phenomenon which exists and cuts across various religious frontiers. You have Christian fundamentalism (which was the original connotation of fundamentalism), Jewish fundamentalism, Islamic fundamentalism, and, of course, now, with the calls for a Hindu raj, Hindu fundamentalism and Buddhist fundamentalism and the like. This phenomenon is a response to the withering effect of a modernistic atmosphere which simply forces religion to withdraw into its own cocoon, into its formal cocoon, and become more and more impervious to its inner dimension with the result of even greater conflict with other religions than existed before.

Now, in such a situation the effect of the presence of the modern world is twofold: One is through the destruction of religion and the other through the foreshortening of its vision. Therefore, those people who are trying to bring about an understanding in the context of religious pluralism and are trying to really reach out and create an understanding with other religions have to meet a double challenge: the challenge of a world which denies the significance of religious categories and the challenge of religious communities which are more and more closed in the face of what they see as threats from the outside. I will cite an example of this situation for you from my own part of the world. In those parts of the Islamic world which have had contact with other religions, as, for example, with Christians in Syria or in Egypt, or with Jews in Iran who did not migrate to Israel, or with Buddhists and Hindus in India (minus of course those affected by the experience of the partition and all that it left in the minds of many people), you would hardly meet any grandfather of the older generation of today who did not have some kind of respect for members of other religious communities. That is, until recently great piety was combined with respect for others even if it was not always accompanied by deep understanding of what the other world was saying.

Today, in contrast, when you look at those young students at an Islamic university who do all the shouting and who think they are the most pious and devout of all Muslims, many of them are the ones who, in contrast to their grandfathers, have much less interest and much less affinity for friendship with people of other religions. The same holds true for other religious worlds. This is a phenomenon which is easy to understand if we consider the externalizing effect of modernism. The proponents of modernism foresaw the gradual dissolution of all religion so that in due course there would be no religion left. Or else they expected new religions would be invented, religions which would be in keeping with the fashions of the day, or that existing religions would be changed in such a way that they would be in conformity with the prevailing trends and would be timely and could be called timely. How wrong they were.

I cannot say more about this issue here, but I need to mention that one of the great tragedies of our times is that in the modern world, especially in America, people have the tendency to absolutize the fashions of each decade. These fashions identified with "absolute values" (however temporary) then become the criteria by which the wisdom of the ages is judged, and then we can go on to the next decade and its new fashions! Right now for those who are affected by such ways of thinking all women in Bangladesh have to be like feminists in New York! Now twenty

years down the road what the women in New York will be doing I do not know. But meanwhile those women in New York
will turn to other concerns in life, other than having to make
their own sexual choices. But those women in Bangladesh who
are supposed to emulate their Western sisters in having to learn
to be concerned primarily with having the freedom to make their
own sexual choices would be out of tune with the times. This of
course is the great tragedy of this age. In this situation we try
to "re-invent" our own religions in order to be timely and fash-
ionable, which of course means the death of the perennial and
traditional reality of religion.

So to come back to the basic argument, the situation today presents us with this remarkable phenomenon, which is in
sharp contrast to what was predicted only twenty-five years ago.
Twenty-five years ago, most social scientists and people who were
studying the sociology of religion and so forth (that is, a combination of the modern social sciences and religious disciplines)
were predicting the increasing dilution of religion. They felt that
the phenomenon which had overtaken the West since the four-
teenth and fifteenth centuries with the coming of nominalism and
which ended with Bertrand Russell's *Why I Am Not a Christian*
was certainly going to be duplicated in the Islamic world and
the Indian world and the Buddhist world. They could not foresee that there could also be this other reaction which would, you
might say, result in a thickening of the outer wall of each religious community which felt itself endangered by the threat of its
destruction by secularist forces and out of this fear each community would try to cut itself off more and more from its own
inner dimension, that dimension which alone provides the way
toward an understanding of other religions. The sad story of the
world today is that the carrying out of serious discourse on pluralism is made difficult not only by the forces of secularism but
also by this new assertion of externalization and particularism,
which denies other religions even against precedents of one's own
religious history.

I will be circumspect and not talk about Christianity, Judaism,
and other religions and will limit myself to Islam, but I am sure
that you could find similar situations across the globe. Take, for

instance, the case of India, where for centuries Hindus and Muslims lived together in relative peace. The very land near the Babri mosque, the mosque which was torn down recently, was given by the Muslim ruler for the building of a Hindu temple, which still stands next door to where the mosque stood. So the destruction of this mosque represents the destruction of centuries of good will and accord. The situation has become much worse in modern times, as compared to medieval times, and people take great pride in believing that people in the twentieth century are now enlightened human beings and beyond religious conflicts! All these claims have turned out to be untrue, but the illusion goes on. The massacre in Bosnia which is called ethnic cleansing has had nothing to do with ethnicity. It has to do with religion. One can never distinguish a Bosnian Muslim from an Orthodox or a Catholic Christian of Bosnia; they all look alike, speak alike, use the same language, have intermarried and lived in the same cities. Now of course we witness the massacre of the Islamic community, and the world plays the violin while Rome burns. This kind of phenomenon is part of the contemporary scene and is far from being something merely medieval.

In the medieval period in the West, the enemy was, of course, branded with pejorative names, religiously speaking, and then attacked. This act is criticized by the modern world as being terrible, and everything one does not like is dubbed as being "medieval." But the fact of the matter is that what was going on during the medieval period often goes on today under other names. Despite the crusades, despite other wars, there were situations such as those in Sicily, Spain, or Portugal where the Christian, Islamic, and Jewish communities lived together in peace for long periods of time. We should never forget that the Inquisition is not a medieval phenomenon. In fact, the expulsion of the Jews and Muslims from Spain did not occur in the Middle Ages. There are some other tragedies which people want to forget today and call them simply "medieval" because many in the West have turned against traditional Christianity, which is identified mostly with the medieval period.

It is different to face fully these realities, as we all know. We are confronted with the situation in which, on the one hand, a lack of understanding of other religions now endangers our attachment to our own religion, and on the other hand, we have new religious phenomena which are opposed to religious pluralism and which enormously complicate the discussion of the reality of religious pluralism. I could address a Muslim audience by reciting again this verse of the Quran and say how un-Quranic it is for any Muslim to disregard the multiplicity of religions, as if God had not been the source of that multiplicity.

Now let me turn back to discuss briefly this question of the *religio perennis* and the inner unity of religions. What is this concept of *religio perennis*, which is at the heart of understanding the plurality of religions? *Religio perennis* means perennial religion, which as I said, is the religious aspect of what is called perennial philosophy or sometimes *sophia perennis*, a term which I favor in some contexts. It is half-Greek, half-Latin but it brings out more than any other term the realized aspect of the *philosophia perennis*. This term is not new; however, its exposition, especially in the writings of Schuon, has new amplitudes and new dimensions which it did not possess in the preceding centuries. But the principle and even the name existed before. Let me again cite for you an Islamic example. There could be parallels in Hinduism and Taoism and other religions of which I am not aware. Of course you have it indirectly in Christianity in the Augustinian doctrine of the Logos. But let me just stick to the Islamic example. Both the Quran and the *Ḥadīth* speak often of the *dīn al-ḥanīf*, the primordial religion. *Ḥanīf* means that which was in the very beginning, perennial and primordial. Eternal and primordial do not have exactly the same meaning, but what is meant is that which was in the very beginning and contains both of these attributes of perennity and primordiality.

As the Quran asserts, Abraham was a Muslim and also *ḥanīfan*; that is, he was a *ḥanīf*, which means pertaining to the primordial state and the primordial monotheism which continued over the ages until the advent of Islam. The term *dīn al-ḥanīf* means precisely *religio perennis*. I was once castigated by someone in Saudi Arabia for talking so much about perennial philosophy, as if this were against Islam. So I recited several *ḥadīths* of the Prophet about the *dīn al-ḥanīf*, and the critic thereafter did not say anything more, for this idea is at the very heart of authentic Islamic doctrine.

Now what does *religio perennis* mean? It is not a religion in addition to other religions. There are not a dozen religions as it were, and a thirteenth one is the *religio perennis*. Rather, it is the reality at the heart of every religion. It is the eternal message of God, the ever-recurring truth at the heart of the diverse manifestations of the Divine Principle. Certain religions do not have a personalistic view of the Divine Principle, such as Taoism or the American Indian religions. But this does not matter. The metaphysical understanding of the *religio perennis* embraces such religions and even Buddhism, which has a nontheistic orientation. Buddhism is based on the doctrine of void, or *śūnyatā*, which manifests itself in such a way that we can assert that it *is* the Divine Principle above and beyond all attributes and particularities. The goal is to reach that Reality or State; otherwise there would be no religion. So whether the Divine Reality is understood in the personalistic or nonpersonalistic sense, it does not really matter. The *religio perennis* believes that all authentic religions issue from the Divine Principle.

This is not to say that all claims to constituting religion are authentic, because these days you can start your own religion. And as I said in the beginning, since nature abhors a vacuum and one of the vacuums created in the modern world has been caused by the intrusion of modernization into the Christian world, this situation has led not only to the introduction of other religions into the West but also to the invention of new religions. The inventive genius of the West is not restricted to the field of computers. Out of California come not only all kinds of new chips from Silicon Valley but also new religions invented practically every few months. Obviously I am not talking about that type of phenomenon. Not everything which we call religion today is authentically religion. You cannot have, as I said, a solution to religious pluralism by including everything and by expecting that the truth claim of religions can be met by putting the truth aside and by saying "Let us all be friends; it does not matter who says what." That has not worked and will never work, yet people keep on saying that it is wonderful to be brotherly and one should love all humanity without need of respecting the truth of other people's religions. But does this sentimental attitude not in fact destroy the claim of the truth upon us? The *religio perennis* does not say that anyone can call anything religion and it therefore becomes religion. It does, however, make possible the inclusion of all the traditional religions which have guided the life of humanity over the ages. It believes that that the Divine Principle has revealed various authentic religious universes. These universes have been revealed according to cosmic laws, in accordance with certain principles, or in Abrahamic language as willed by God, and not ad hoc. God has willed certain religions to be revealed at certain times. And God has willed that in fact there would be no other plenary manifestation after a particular historical moment until the end of time.

There are cosmic laws which determine the conditions of the manifestation of various sacred universes which we call religions. Some religions are meant for small collectivities, some for large ones; some possess wide adaptability and some less so. They are like different kinds of trees. They all have their roots sunk in the Divine Nature, and they all grow according to laws which are determined by the roots. It is true that if you plant a poplar tree here in Illinois it will not be exactly like one in Colorado; there are changes depending on what kind of soil you have, what kind of air, etc. But what grows will still be a poplar tree. It is likewise true that all of these great religions have adapted themselves to different circumstances and climates. Japanese Buddhism and Sri Lankan Buddhism are not identical, but both are nevertheless Buddhism. The same is true of Islam and of Christianity. There are no two human types as different as Spaniards and Russians from the point of view of temperament and psychological makeup, yet they are both Christians. Religions live and adapt themselves to different climates while also molding their climate and even perish from the earth according to laws determined by their roots that are sunk in the Divine Nature, just as the tree grows according to certain laws. And like the tree a religion can wither away. It will, however, never die like a tree because a religion returns to its celestial prototype even if it ceases to be a living reality here on earth. Furthermore, it must be remembered that we cannot give new life to the sacred tree of religion once its earthly life has been taken away by God. We cannot reinvent a religion that was very much living centuries ago, a millennium ago, by just studying its external symbols and forms or reenacting its rites. That is not going to bring it back to life. There is a divine life and there is the life of the spirit within these sacred forms which at a particular moment in the cycle of life of a religion can leave it. In such cases we are left with beautiful works of art, with symbols, with books, but the rites are no longer efficacious, and indeed you might say that grace is lacking and the angels are no longer around to participate in uplifting us through the performance of those sacred rites.

It is in the light of its celestial prototype that the traditional perspective and the *religio perennis* envisage the essential reality of each religion. The traditional perspective also believes that each religion must participate in the particularity for which it was destined and must embrace the whole life of its followers. Religion is not simply a Sunday-morning affair. It is the unfortunate marginalization of Christianity in the last few centuries that has made many people think that what is now observable in many areas in the West is religion as it should be. If you lived in Italy in the thirteenth century, every day of the year was occupied by religion. And how tragic that just forty years ago (when I was a graduate student at Harvard) I still had many Catholic friends who went to church three times a day, like Muslims praying five times a day, but even that has now become rare. This separation of religion from the whole of life is a result not of the structure of Christianity but of the impact in the West of an ever encroaching secularism that denies to religion its legitimate rights. But religion itself is for the whole of life, and therefore from the point of view of the *religio perennis,* from the point of view of *sophia perennis,* everything in the universe of religion traditionally understood is sacred. The forms are sacred and the doctrines are sacred. They are not just simply later historical accretions which we throw away with the psychological certitude that we know better. Nor are they simply human responses to the call of the Divine. How many people today think that they know much better than Saint Thomas Aquinas what God was saying, and therefore have thrown away Thomism in the name of the philosophies of the twentieth century, philosophies which they are parading around as theology! And the same is now happening in Hinduism and gradually in Islam, Buddhism, and other religions, and certainly in Judaism, which has suffered the same kind of attack.

In contrast to all the currents of relativism, historicism, and deconstruction of religions and sacred scriptures, the traditionalist perspective which emphasizes the *religio perennis* believes that each sacred universe is sacred not only in the inner meaning lying at its very *heart* but in the forms which have been revealed. Within that sacred tradition there accumulates over the ages what the Catholics call *traditio,* and every tradition has something like that, something which accumulates over the ages like the various branches of the tree which grow up from the trunk. Now we are sitting on one of those branches. We are not sitting on the trunk and we can have no relation to the roots except through the branches and the trunk; to think otherwise is to betray the reality of the tree and our own situation. So the traditional understanding of religion, in contrast to all of these critiques of religion by various forms of modernity (which in fact consider modernity as an absolute and religion as something relative), has tried to preserve the integral nature of each religion and sacred tradition. From the other side it has opposed adamantly, within each of those sacred universes, the absolutization of what is relative within that sacred universe.

This brings out a very difficult metaphysical issue which I cannot discuss in full here but to which I must return: the sense of the absolute in each religion. It is true that if one is a pious Christian, Jew, Muslim, or Hindu, one goes to a church, synagogue, mosque, or temple to pray to the Divinity to perform rites grounded in the Divine and possessing a sense of absoluteness. What these people are doing is experienced by them to be absolute; otherwise they would not perform it. When I get up in the morning, I say *"Allāhu akbar"* (God is the greatest) in the direction of the *qiblah*. If it did not really matter to God, and this matter were relative, I could face New York instead and do or say something else. That, however, I would never do as a Muslim.

I would simply not do such a thing because of the "absolute-ness" of the Islamic injunctions concerning the daily prayers. The demand of the sacred on us, which must involve all of our be-ing, comes from that absoluteness within religion and responds to our own thirst for the Absolute which is deeply rooted in the substance of human nature. Human beings cannot live with pure relativity. And that is why when they are cut off from the real Absolute, they absolutize the relative as we now see around us all the time and in nearly every domain.

Now, traditional or perennial philosophy and the *religio peren-nis* insist that every authentic religion comes from the Absolute and there is the sense of absoluteness in it. Moreover, there are levels of the manifestation of the Absolute which are themselves "absolute" within the universe created by the particular religion in question. Again, this truth is beautifully expressed by Frithjof Schuon in the concept of the "relatively absolute," that which is not the Absolute as such but is relatively absolute within a par-ticular religious universe. This is the heart of the matter: how to understand and respect other religions in terms of absoluteness and truth. Let me give you an example, again starting with my own tradition in order not to offend anybody and also because I cannot be an authority on all religions, certainly not more au-thoritative than the many eminent scholars from other religions present here.

Within the Islamic tradition, the Absolute, *al-muṭlaq* in Ara-bic, is Allah alone. Only the one God, the Supreme Reality, is absolute, and not even the Divine Names and Qualities which still belong to the divine level of reality are the Absolute as such, the Absolute being one. God has ninety-nine Names, and their very multiplicity shows that they belong to the domain of rela-tivity (albeit divine relativity), if one understands what relativity means metaphysically. It is only the Divine Essence, the Divine One, *al-Aḥad,* who is *muṭlaq,* who is absolute. But in the every-day life of Islam, the Quran is also absolute on its own level as the final Word of God. The injunctions of the *Sharī'ah* or the Divine Law are also absolute on their own level, because the *Sharī'ah* is also the law of God; otherwise one would not follow it. I could go down the list of many other realities of such nature.

In the case of Christianity again, the same truth can be observed. It is true that Western Christianity has absolutized the trinitarian relationship, but to talk about three is to be already in the domain of relationality. So in a sense for Christians the Trinity is the "relatively absolute" at the highest level. What is absolutely absolute is the Godhead. But then within the Christian world Christ is also absolute. He is the only son of God, and many Christians, in fact, take the saying of Christ, "I am the way, the truth, and the life, he who shall follow me shall have life everlasting," as proof that all other religions are false. Of course, Christ did not say the only way, the only truth, the only life. That interpretation was usually added by the later commentators who wanted to denigrate other religions. In any case, here the Absolute again descends like a cascade from the highest metaphysical level of the Absolute in Itself to various levels, finally coming down to the Eucharist, which on its own level is again absolute for Christians, for it is the celebration of the rite promulgated by Christ. You cannot have a man-made rite, that is an absurdity. All divine rites, according to the *religio perennis,* come from God, from the Sun Dance, to the Eucharist, to the Muslim daily prayers, to the *pujas,* whatever they are in the various religions. And therefore you have, you might say, a cascading of absoluteness which, if understood metaphysically, does not at all destroy the character of absoluteness even within the world of relativity. Were we to understand this cardinal concept, we could preserve the sense of absoluteness and "absolute truth" in our own religion while understanding why other religions also make claims to absoluteness in ways other than our own. What is essential is never to forget that only the Absolute is absolute but that there are realities which are "relatively absolute" within a particular religious universe.

Let me give you an astronomical example. The sun for us is absolute in our solar system; it is the only sun. And anyone who acts as if it were otherwise becomes psychologically imbalanced. If we got up every morning thinking that there are many suns in the solar system wandering in space thousands of miles a second along with our own solar system we would become mentally sick. Our imaginal faculty relegates that thought to the realm of theoretical knowledge, which is not relevant existentially. Somebody used to say jokingly, when I was in Harvard, that the conception of intergalactic space in modern astronomy is the reason why so many modern astronomers do not feel mentally normal. That hyperbole seems a bit strange, but it implies that because they deal so much with intergalactic space and abstract themselves from terrestrial space, they no longer feel totally at home in the human space. For us, in this human space on earth, our sun is *the* sun, but from the point of view of intergalactic astronomy, it is just *a* sun. Now its being *a* sun does not negate its being *the* sun in our planetary system. It is this central symbol which is essential for the understanding of the claim of the perennial philosophy and the *religio perennis* in respect to absoluteness in each sacred universe, without denying that, in fact, only the Absolute is absolute.

This latter doctrine is expressed beautifully in Arabic as *al-Tawḥīdu wāḥid:* the doctrine of oneness is unique. There cannot be two Ones; there is only *the* One. Everything other than the One is already the descent of the One toward a particular sacred universe. To be able to discern the levels of absoluteness in various religious worlds is more of an art than a science. The practice of this great art also needs divine confirmation in order for us to be able to penetrate into other religious universes, to be able to locate the various levels of the manifestations of the Absolute within each universe and therefore be able to respect them for what they are within that universe. This art is never based on a one-to-one equivalence, although there are always easily discernible correspondences. In a religion such as Islam or Judaism, the sacred book is central. In a religion such as Christianity, the book is important but it is the person of Christ who is central. In Buddhism, the Buddha is central, and Pali texts take a second place. In certain religions, certain practices are one way; in other religions, they follow other ways. Even when it comes to the question of sacred law, in certain religions such as Judaism, Hinduism, and Islam, the sacred law is directly revealed: the *Halakah,* the Laws of Manu, the *Sharī'ah,* and so on. In others such as Christianity the sacred law is summarized through a general set of spiritual laws as expounded by Christ, especially in the Sermon on the Mount, which is a spiritual testament but which does not tell you how to sell your goods in the bazaar. These laws do not concern themselves with the particulars of everyday life as do the laws of Judaism, Hinduism, and Islam. Such a possibility does, however, exist, as we see so clearly in the case of Christianity.

What is difficult for us human beings to do is to transcend precisely this tendency, which is part of human nature, to always desire to see in others exactly as we are ourselves. A simple Muslim would say: "But how is it that Christians eat pork? Did not Christ accept the Laws of Moses? Some of these later Christians have become confused. Why are they eating pork?" They make this criticism even if they have Armenian or Orthodox friends who come to their house for dinner in Syria and Lebanon or Coptic friends in Egypt who do not abstain from eating pork. Ordinary Muslims cannot understand such a fact; for it is in the nature of most human beings to see others in their likeness. Look at the polemic of Christianity against Islam for nine hundred years since Peter the Venerable ordered the Quran to be translated into Latin and there arose the concern about why it is that it permits polygamy if it is a revealed book. Christians believed that since they practiced monogamy, it had to be an absolute moral law which was sacred. Anybody who practiced anything other than that must therefore be wrong. There are many other examples which could be given coming down to our own days.

We act and think as if we know better than Christ or the Prophet of Islam or the *avatars* of Vishnu. What we are saying or what we are doing in judging other religions is precisely because of this human frailty of always trying to see others in our own light. It cannot be denied that on the human level, when traditions have been strong, the sense of seeing the sacred in other traditions has seeped into everyday life even if one has not understood the metaphysical foundations of other religions. There is no doubt about that. When the Muslims came to India, many of the simple Hindus saw great sanctity in the Sufis. Many Muslims also revered certain Hindus because of the presence of sanctity within them. There are thousands of stories bearing witness to this fact, and they are also found within other religions in medieval times. Saint John of the Cross, one of the greatest of all Christian mystical poets and the greatest poet of the Spanish language, went to Granada as a young man, and there he met an old Morisco woman who remained secretly a Muslim and who taught him much of what he knew. This is how he came to learn about Arabic Sufi poetry, which is reflected in some of the symbols that he used — not that the adoption of such teachings made him any less a great saint of the Christian Church. Saint John said that in the woman's presence he felt the presence of wisdom, the presence of sanctity. This presence of the sacred in other religious forms was also felt on the popular level; there is no doubt about it. But people did not understand it in depth.

The sacred is like perfume: once you have a nose for it you can smell it, and once you have a sense of the sacred you know which religions have guarded their sacred character, which have become weakened, which have become distorted, and which are simply pseudo-religions and man-made fads parading as religion. It is like those people in France who are employed to smell good perfume and who have done so for years; as soon as they open the bottle of perfume and smell it they can judge its quality and do not need to do anything else. To live religion fully, to have had an experience of the sacred, gives human beings the criterion for experiencing the sacred elsewhere. That is not what is difficult if we have a sense of the sacred ourselves. It is the intellectual, theological, and philosophical understanding which today is unfortunately rare but is difficult to come by while at the same time being needed more than ever before. I say "unfortunately" precisely because human beings have not been created to live in several spiritual universes, except for those rare men and women who have already transcended forms, those who not only talk about transcending forms, but who have really transcended them.

The normal situation is to have one's religion, one's particular sacred tradition, like having one's own family, village, town, or language. How many people can compose poetry in three languages? It is an extremely rare thing even to be a master of one's own mother tongue, and if one is gifted, one can be a good poet in one's own tongue. Religion is like that, and therefore I say "unfortunately" because of the incredible challenge that God has put before us in our having to take seriously religions other than our own. But this situation is not only a challenge; it could also be a remarkable benediction from Heaven. It is a gift from Heaven because it can help us to avoid the destruction of our own religious universe. It is the awareness of the sacred wherever it manifests itself and the possibility of confirming the presence of the sacred in other religions while remaining firmly rooted in our own which has to be emphasized so that pluralism can become the source not of the destruction but of accord and confirmation of the universality of religion in the face of all the secularizing forces which seek to destroy all religions. To bring about this transformation we should at least learn from the errors of the last hundred years since Vivekananda spoke in this city.

What should we learn? First of all, that the rejection of all religions in the name of human accord, humanism, progress, and all of the gods of the nineteenth century only weakens authentic religion without solving human problems. The greatest wars of this century were not fought between Serbs and Croats within Christianity or between Bosnian Muslims and Croats, although that is horrendous enough, but between two different interpretations of Marxism or between, of course, fascism and communism in Europe, which killed about 30 million people. And so we have had that experience and know that the rejection of religion does not imply the end of human conflict. Nobody who is serious about the issue will entertain the idea that the problem of pluralism can be solved by simply neglecting the reality of religion or of weakening it into an amorphous lowest common denominator. Religion is in the nature of human beings. To be human is to also to seek to be more than human, as Saint Augustine said, and to try to be more than human is to try to breach the wall of the suffocating world of our own ego, and therefore to be in quest of religion which alone can save us from our own ego-centeredness. If we cannot find the real thing, we will find the fake one, but it is in our nature to search for it. That is one lesson we must learn from the experience of the last century, namely, that religious pluralism is not and cannot be solved by simply denying all religions or reducing them to what *we* consider to be important.

Second, we cannot substitute the kingdom of man for the kingdom of God, to use a Christian term. To say that human beings come first, to say let us just have peace and let each person "do his or her own thing," is totally absurd from a traditional point of view and is against the nature of things. Why should God allow us to live at peace while forgetting him? Why should God waste his creation, if this creation has any meaning? After denying the meaning of that creation, why should we have peace? So the idea of a kind of abstract peace irrespective of the truth will never work, and again I think the experiences of the last century should have taught us that lesson concerning this matter. But it is so difficult for human beings to learn such lessons.

And finally, the assertion that only my religion is true and all other religions are false, while it is acceptable on a certain level, should be left on that level; it cannot be acceptable when various religions meet each other. A simple farmer two hundred miles from here in the middle of Iowa, living in a completely Lutheran community, might not have had any serious contact with another religion. He does not have to spend his time reading Patañjali's *Yogasutra* or the *Tao Te Ching*. It would be enough for him to be a good Christian and God would be pleased. But if one is in an ambience in which contact is made with other religions, with other communities, with other humanities, this kind of attitude can be religiously suicidal. This is again one of the great trials of our times: that what was a perfectly normal human attitude for other periods of history is now so dangerous for many who live in a multireligious world. But we have an environment in which so many things that people did normally for a long time, like cutting trees and burning them in winter, are no longer viable. If all the Chinese did that for a few years there would be no trees left in all of China. The global situation has changed, and therefore we also must address ourselves to this condition. To do that we have to be able to pray to God to enable us to see the One in the many and the many as reflected in the One, to have the sense of the truth in various sacred universes and to learn from those whom God has given the knowledge to guide us in this field, as the more traditional humanities did over the ages, listening to their own sages and seers when they spoke about such matters. Now, however, this has to be done in a more general fashion. As for those of us who cannot do that, we should always remember that all of our religions teach respect and tolerance for other people even if we do not understand them. And therefore let me end with the quotation from the Quran with which I began: "So vie with one another in good works. Unto God will ye be brought back, and He will inform you about that wherein ye differed."*

---

*This chapter is based on the oral presentation made by the author.

Chapter 9

Summation: Call to Action

Robert J. Schreiter

This concluding session has been advertised as summary remarks and as a call to action. Let me say a little bit about that before I get under way with that task. First of all, in terms of summary remarks, I do not intend to give a chronicle of the marvelous presentations we have heard and the discussions that we have engaged in over these last several days. What I am going to try to do is bring together some of the recurring ideas and themes that have threaded their way through this consultation, this conference. Some of these threads, of course, were planned. As Jeffrey Carlson indicated, the research committee and the parliament have been working on this conference for quite a number of years, and so it is not surprising that some of this does come together.

Secondly, I want to touch upon some of the salient ideas and the challenges that were placed before us by the speakers, by the respondents, by the conversation, and try to answer the question: Have we here together in this conference moved the discussion of religious pluralism to a new place? Are we in a different place now than we were when we began? I need to say something also about the call to action that is advertised in the program. I think it was the poet Horace who coined the phrase *habent sua fata libelli,* that books have their own destiny, they have their own fate. Anyone who has written a book knows that; you think you said one thing, but people pay no attention to that and they grab onto something else. Well, to paraphrase Horace: *habent sua fata congressus,* conferences undergo a particular fate as well. When this conference first began to be organized we were instructed by the parliament to have a call-to-action section. In the meantime I think we are about the only survivor of that early planning that has actually kept to the pattern. So what I will be doing is less than giving a stirring call to action. I will note some of the important things that have come out. A number of our speakers have done that for us, and I present these as an opportunity for us to discuss and explore them further when these remarks are concluded.

Finally, by way of introduction, a few disclaimers. As was indicated, I have been one of the planners of this conference. Probably there are fewer people in a worse position than a planner to sum up because of the danger of hearing what I want to hear. I'll try to overcome that as best I can, but those of you who have said different things in this process, please amplify my remarks as we move along. Second, in a theme that Seyyed Hossein Nasr touched upon again and again this morning, I am a Westerner, one of those people who are particularly inclined to ponder the issues of religious pluralism. Moreover, a lot of my comments about where this might go are going to be centered not only on the West but upon this country. The United States is now the second most multicultural country in the world, surpassed only by Australia. So it becomes in many ways a crucible for the kinds of questions of pluralism that virtually every country around the world has to deal with these days. I don't apologize for doing that, but at the same time, I want to keep an attentive edge in that regard. And finally, like all of us here, I hope, I have my own commitments to these kinds of questions. Those will probably become evident as I go along. What I would like to do, as a way of trying to weave together the sorts of things we have been talking about over these last several days, is to present it under five headings.

The first will deal with the contexts in which we talk about pluralism: what context urges us into these kinds of discussions? Second, I want to look at the modes of response: what are the resources we use to respond to the reality of pluralism in our midst? Third, I want to take up some of the major issues — these are those salient points I was referring to before, salient points that I think we need to continue to ponder. Fourth, in an attempt to answer the question of whether we have moved to a new place; I want to look at some of the remapping, if you will, of the terrain that has been going on in the midst of this conference: suggestions for new definitions, or alternative definitions, to help us better understand what we are, how we are situated, and where we are going in the midst of pluralism. And then finally number five, to look to the future — this is where all those call-to-action questions are going to collect themselves.

Contexts

So, first, the context of pluralism. I believe that contexts are important: they do not determine a situation. But if you do not pay attention to them, then they're likely to take over. The more we know about the context of our discussion, the better we will be able to concentrate on what we are particularly concerned about. Four sets of contexts have been particularly important in our discussions in this conference.

The first is the context of modernity. This has been referred to in various ways in the course of the presentations; it has been talked about as a Western point of view; we heard Seyyed Hossein Nasr talk about it in this fashion. It was spoken of as the Enlightenment paradigm by people like Raimon Panikkar. Whatever we call it, it has been front and center in our discussions here. Virtually all of the participants have looked at modernity in a critical fashion. I am not aware of anybody who has simply embraced it uncritically. Perhaps the person most critical of it was Nasr, who, in his remarks, comes the closest, perhaps, of anybody to either rejecting or ignoring the presence of modernity. To him it seemed an almost unalloyed set of bad news. Raimon Panikkar, in his opening address, set up a marvellous kind of dialectic in looking at modernity by, on the one hand, emphasizing the need to hold on to a sense of mystery but at the same time insisting that we cannot sacrifice rationality. One of the great gifts of modernity is one style of rationality that does allow us to look closely and critically at things. Arthur Waskow kept talking about how modernity has brought us to the edge of the abyss and provided a number of models for that on a perhaps more positive but nonetheless critical note. His respondent, Ali Jaffrey of the Zoroastrian community, looked at the opportunities that modernity raised for the renewal of his own tradition. I would like to add my own voice here to this discussion about modernity as a context. We cannot not deal with modernity. We cannot afford to simply ignore it or reject it. It will sneak around behind us and come right at us when we least expect it. We cannot reject it; we cannot avoid it. We have to come to terms with the reality of modernity. Many people are sounding the end of the modern period or at least express the wistful hope that such might be the case. But we need to examine this attitude critically, because modernity has also given us a very powerful set of tools for looking at pluralism itself. And so we cannot simply do away with it.

A second context that has played a major role in our discussions here is ethnicity. This has to do with the migration of peoples around the world. Perhaps the most graphic, indeed stunning, presentation on that was given to us by Diana Eck with her slide shows and with her statistics about particularly how the face of America has changed since the Asian Immigration Act of 1965. This has brought in new waves of people and created a new pluralism in our society. In certain parts of the country, particularly the West Coast, there is no ethnic majority anymore; no one is in the majority, all represent a faction of a minority. Also, although she did not use the exact language, at the heart of her project lay the issue of what it means to be ethnic. If you live in Mexico, were born in Mexico, and grew up in Mexico, you are simply a Mexican. However, if you migrate, say to the United States, you become a member of an ethnic group. What I mean is that you have to relate to another culture and take on an awareness about your own culture in a way that would not be the case if you are in a majority and don't need to attend to that kind of thing. One of the things that Diana Eck's presentation particularly reminded us all about is that our identities are in flux. She used one very graphic example of the consecration of a new Hindu temple in Pittsburgh, and how all the people in the Indian community took part in this two-week ceremony. One of the striking things about this, she pointed out, was that had this happened in India, almost none of the people present would have been part of it. But now the consecration of this temple is part of the warp and woof of the identity and the continuance of the Indian community. We see this over and over again in this country.

I mentioned Mexico. In the Mexican community in this city, people who were perhaps only casually observant of religious festivals at home become intensely involved here because it is now tied up much more with their sense of identity. This reminds us that not only is the identity of those people who are immigrating into this setting changing; the identity of those who have been here a long time is also being changed. An example struck me while I was going out of the hotel after the last session: down on the street level, there is a little stand in the corridor dishing out pizza. One needs to realize that thirty-five years ago only people of southern Italian heritage would even have known what a pizza was! Now it is just simply American food. In fact, while it is considered somewhat embarrassedly by Italians as peasant food — it is basically dough topped with whatever you have — now they are quite proud of this cultural achievement that they've exported to the United States. There is no Archimedean point. The language of decentering figured regularly into this conference. What this means, and Panikkar particularly touched on this, is that some of the boundaries we thought were rather clear in identifying ourselves and others take on a much more fluid character. We start to realize the kind of flux that we are in all the time.

A third context of pluralism that figures into our discussions — and this, of course, consciously so — was that of globalization. Globalization is both a good thing and a bad thing. It is a good thing because it enhances the ability to communicate, it breaks down barriers in important kinds of ways. This was simply not the case before. One of the best examples is what is going on right now in China with the introduction of satellite dishes. This will do more to change the country quickly than any change of government. And recently Rupert Murdoch has bought Star TV in the hopes of beaming a whole set of programs specifically aimed at China. My favorite example of how globality has changed so many things is the following one. There is a large refugee camp south of Mexico City, full of refugees coming out of Guatemala

and El Salvador. When the king and queen of Spain visited Mexico a number of years ago, the people who were in charge of
that refugee camp wanted to bring to their attention the plight of
the people in those camps. Needless to say, they were prevented
by phalanxes of guards and bureaucrats from ever getting close
to the king and queen until they came up with the obvious solution: they got hold of the fax number of the king's suite and
simply faxed him the information. There is nobody who could
stop that, and the king and queen actually did come and visit the
camp. So globality is a good thing in that sort of way that we
can move around, that we can gather as we are gathering here in
this parliament so much more easily than was the case a hundred
years ago.

But it is also a bad thing. It is overwhelming many smaller
communities. Globalization in many parts of the world means
fighting off the creation of what's been called McWorld, a world
dominated by American cultural icons, entertainment, and food.
That, to be sure, is interpreted differently in different places, but
at the same time it is leading us in ways, perhaps, that we do
not want to go. So it is both a good thing and a bad thing,
but it has become a context that makes, along with ethnicity, the
issue of pluralism an inevitable one for us all, not simply something that fascinates or stimulates the imagination of intellectuals
but a day-to-day kind of happening. In one of the workshops
connected with this conference, the Reverend Sunnan Kubose
talked about what happened when he and his family moved into
Skokie. He was in charge of the Buddhist temple of Chicago.
His neighbors, very pious Christians, were very concerned about
having Buddhists next door. He got in a conversation one day
in the backyard over the fence with his neighbor. She was kind
of worried about how all this was going to work out. Kubose
then had the good fortune to say, "Well, I'd rather have a good
Buddhist then a bad Christian as a neighbor." And, as a result of that, they've become good friends. But we are all now
part of this bigger mix; we simply cannot escape it. And, indeed, it is creating new realities. Someone in the discussion of
Diana Eck's presentation noted that among the other computer
networks you can sign on to now is On-line Sangha, which is

linking up the Buddhist communities around the country, the
Dharmanet.

The fourth set of contexts that is shaping pluralism has to do
with conflict and suffering. We tend to try to look at the pluralism question as some kind of homeostatic model. Samuel Ruiz
reminded us that conflict is simply part of life and is experienced
as central to life by the poor and the oppressed of this world.
Paul Knitter likewise focused upon the centrality of suffering as
the hermeneutical key of genuinely understanding the other. Conflict is simply part of the fabric of life. For many people there
is a history of conflict. Perhaps most eloquently it was Gurinder
Singh Mann who talked about the experiences of the encounter
between Hindus, Muslims, and Sikhs. For the Sikh community,
that story now has become *the* story that is basically held together with metaphors of conflict and violence. And one of the
struggles in that community is to find alternative models, other
metaphors upon which to build the story of what it has meant
to be a Sikh. So conflict and suffering question the very framework, the very context itself, in which we try to imagine what
the realities of pluralism are going to be like.

Modes of Response

In turning to the second area — the modes of response to the reality of pluralism in our world — I would like to highlight four that
kept weaving and threading their way through our conversations.
The first set of responses or modes of response were philosophical
ones. We have been looking for an overarching frame that would
help us, guide us, through the discussion of pluralism. I think
this was a particularly salient characteristic of Raimon Panikkar's
presentation. He tried to equip us, as it were, with a language
that would help us understand the plurality and indeed the pluralism of our world. Similarly, Seyyed Hossein Nasr early on in
his presentation insisted upon the importance of a well-thought-
out and adequate metaphysical framework for approaching the
whole matter of pluralism. Those are some of the positive aspects of that kind of a response. We were also reminded by both
Panikkar and Nasr of the negative side of the philosophical mode

of response, namely, that philosophical modes of response can be used to deconstruct religious identity. They can be used as a way to actually pull apart religious identity in such a way that it cannot be put back together again. This remains particularly true of some Enlightenment forms of philosophy. Likewise, philosophical approaches highlight certain points of departure. Again Panikkar talked about this principally in the form of two models: a monistic model in which ultimately all reality has to be construed and grasped as one, or a dualistic model in which there are two elements that are involved, raising the question of commensurability. That is to say: is the reality of the world such that all seeming pluralities can be resolved, can be reduced? And he suggested that they cannot be so reduced, that there are irreducible differences in the world. A second mode of response that figured, of course, very strongly in the discussion of religious pluralism were religious or theological responses for those in the theistic traditions. Again, Nasr perhaps placed the most emphasis on the particularity of traditions by invoking the work of Frithjof Schuon on the perennial nature of religion that rises above all religious traditions, that there is a perennial sense of religion of which the different religions are manifestations. Panikkar offered some other possibilities, again very specific to his principal tradition. He spoke as a Christian employing a Christological paradigm of self-emptying as a way to understand other traditions. Ronald Kidd in his response to Paul Knitter suggested yet another, the importance of the path, in the sense not so much of being guided by a concept or an idea or a reality such as God, but as a path along which one goes and in so going discovers the way. It is important, I think, to pay attention to Nasr's caveats. We cannot sacrifice our truth claims in order to get along in a pluralistic world; we must remain faithful to our traditions, but as the other contexts have suggested, no tradition simply stands there in one place. A living tradition, as Panikkar particularly pointed out, is constantly in movement and in flux and that has to be discerned as well.

The third set of responses were ethical, perhaps phrased most clearly by Paul Knitter and Bishop Samuel Ruiz. Knitter called for a praxis-based understanding of religious pluralism and the role of dialogue within that. They noted the necessity of action, that there must be more than words: it must be action. Similarly, Samuel Ruiz spoke of the voices of the poor and the hermeneutical privilege that they have in helping us interpret reality. The primacy of the ethical has asserted itself especially strongly in recent years in interreligious dialogue. The very fact that at this Parliament of the World's Religion discussion is going on about a declaration of a global ethic rather than a search for harmony in other kinds of ways I think points to this.

Finally, a fourth set of responses has to do with the fact that ultimately we stand before mystery, that our concepts never embrace our symbols and our symbols never exhaust the mystery of which they speak. Panikkar again struck this note particularly strongly, as did this morning Masao Abe. That this is an important thing simply cannot be forgotten. For us, particularly those in the United States with its culture dominated by European history, it might be good here to evoke once again Gabriel Marcel, the French philosopher, if I may paraphrase him: "That religious pluralism is not [so much] a problem to be solved as a mystery to be lived." And we tend to think of it often as a problem, and if we can only get the solution right we'll move on to something else. Rather, as a number of our speakers have indicated, it is an invitation to participate in a mystery, a mystery that in turn will transform us.

Issues

We turn now to issues. What were some of the big issues that have arisen in this conference? I would like to concentrate on four of them. The first is: For whom is religious pluralism an issue or a problem? Seyyed Hossein Nasr suggests that this is largely a Western problem. I would beg to disagree with him on that. I think it has gone far beyond that, if for no other reason than that the migration of peoples has created this as a problem everywhere. Let me give you just one example. It has more to do with culture than difference in religion, but it highlights the issue. I was talking recently to a man in Japan who is a pastor. He was saying that one of the principal issues within his congregation is that Japanese Christians (Roman Catholics in this instance) have struggled so hard to create an identity as a tiny minority in a much larger community. And now they are confronted with the reality of Filipino workers who have been imported into Japan and now constitute almost half the congregation! And so they had to deal with yet another set of issues that they didn't have to before. Repeated instances of this kind of thing can be found, I think, over and over around the world. So the issue of religious pluralism is not just for Westerners anymore. Westerners may have a sense of having been alerted to it first, but I think, as I will suggest at the end, we need to look at some of the models of other kinds of encounter through history and in different places to help us understand and perhaps free up our vision in this regard.

Second, in terms of for whom it is a problem, is it a problem primarily for liberals? People who, as Nasr suggested, may have lost a great deal of their religious faith? In another kind of context, I have heard a prominent sociologist of religion in this country say that the two most interesting things going on today in the world of religion are the rise of Pentecostal Christianity and Muslim fundamentalism, and neither of these groups is really much in evidence at this parliament! As Harvey Cox reminded us this morning, to speak in general terms about Evangelicals who are not interested in interreligious dialogue, is simply to generalize about the other. Like Professor Cox, I work a great deal in those circles and know that finer differentiations are required than "Evangelical." That does not even begin to cover a wide spectrum of Christianity. Moreover, it is perhaps just a liberal notion that these people are not interested in these questions. Many of them are. I think it is important to realize, therefore, that these are not just issues that stimulate or fascinate the liberal imagination because, again, it is part of the reality in which we live and it is a reality that we all share. Raising the question of for whom is this a problem has a distinct value, I believe, in reminding us that we need to be sensitive to boundaries and perspectives. To that extent we would be more effective in the discussion. So that is one issue. The second, third, and fourth issues are the three subthemes of this conference, namely, identity, conflict, and globality.

I think perhaps the most important area that emerged here, for me at least, is that even though the word *identity* comes from the word *idem*, in Latin, which means the same, as one of our speakers reminded us, identity is no longer the same. In some instances, we talk of multiple identities. Julia Ching, both a Chinese Canadian and a Confucian Catholic, has shown us that the issue of multiple identity is a strong one. Professor Panikkar, who claims at least three major religious identities, stated that identity can not be seen perhaps in terms of a monistic model anymore, that it has to be seen at least dialogically if not in much more complex kinds of ways. I think what was particularly powerful in this conference were some of the narratives, the stories that we heard, of people dealing with their identity. I'm thinking of three in particular: Julia Ching and the discussion of what it meant to move from China via the United States and then to Canada. Her respondent, Hoda Mahmoudi is a Baha'i; her father was Baha'i, and her mother was Muslim but became Baha'i. This created struggles in terms of identity and place and belonging, and then she moved from Iran, where she was born, to Utah, which is no more hospitable to Baha'is than Iran. Arthur Waskow talked about it in terms of a struggle, a wrestling that one goes through in order to be faithful to a tradition but yet engage the world in which we live. He talked particularly about a book that he has written with his brother on this question of struggling. The third issue is conflict. What I think the speakers who engaged this question particularly — again Samuel Ruiz, Paul Knitter, Gurinder Singh Mann — is that conflict is not a peripheral issue in our world. It is not something that crops up from time to time, but needs to be seen much more at the heart of these discussions. It is not, in other words, a problem to be solved. And I think it also points out that we have to remap the territory to see how we can understand pluralism in light of that fact. As Ruiz pointed out, it is the fear of conflict that often keeps us from addressing pluralism more directly: both the inner conflicts that it may cause within ourselves and the conflicts it might cause between communities.

The final issue is of globality. I have already mentioned its inevitable character. I think some other things, which were just along the edges of what we talked about, bear further discussion, such as the relationship of globality to universality; Nasr raised this issue particularly in his major address. Are there universals and how are they held together? The postmoderns say there are none. A tradition, or at least the reading of a tradition, such as that of Dr. Nasr, would beg to differ. So what is the relationship of this reality we call globality to the quest for universality and for the quest for unity, the question that Dr. Panikkar raised for us? One other aspect of globality and pluralism was raised again particularly by Paul Knitter with great force, when he reminded us that this is the only earth we have and therefore there are certain things that we simply cannot escape, we cannot get away from.

Remapping

The fourth area I need to talk about is remapping. In this respect three points have emerged out of this conference. The first pertains to what we mean by pluralism, how we define it. Defining means to mark off the boundaries. There seems to be widespread agreement that it is not simply plurality, that pluralism involves an engagement with the other or the others, nor is it simply tolerance. As one of the speakers said, if tolerance is all that we can get, well, let's at least hold on to that. But we need to go beyond tolerance because tolerance can be a very passive kind of thing. I also think that two other points are much in evidence, namely, the importance of looking at particularity, not simply as an instance of the universal but in its own contours and, with that, the sense of irreducibility, namely, that ultimately the religious traditions are not commensurate with one another, that perhaps a majority of the world's languages do not even have a word for what we call religion.

A second type of remapping going on these days is the rethinking of our sense of identity, what we mean when we talk about identity. Diana Eck by showing us the slides of the places where people of different traditions come together to worship and to pray, made the point that nobody and nothing are really as they seem anymore, that from the outside of many buildings you could not tell that it was a house of worship, or, in other instances, it often looked like something else. One picture was a particularly good one, I think. It was a picture from Queens of a building that had been a church, a synagogue, a mortuary, and is now a Sikh house of worship. Appearances are misleading, and sometimes our first mode of identification and classification does not reach far enough. Arvind Sharma in his response, especially to Diana Eck, talked about how we gain identity. Is it conferred on us by others? This is something that often happens in minority communities, in ethnic communities. The majority community decides what a community means. Do we assert an identity of our own? Or what is the relationship of the dialectic between the two? Sharma presented a brief model that I think is worth pursuing. Julia Ching, in the narrative of her own life, talked about how those boundaries had shifted for her, that at one point she felt almost schizoid, having two identities, and then there was a sense that there are multiple layers that somehow mysteriously communicate. Indeed, the question of how many identities we have was raised by both Panikkar and by Julia Ching. Panikkar also had a rider on one of his points that we did not really pursue as well as we might or could have: the relationship of identity to belonging. In some of the research that I am familiar with about why communities continue to assert their ethnic roots even as these become more and more attenuated, of what it means to be part of particular community coming from elsewhere, a lot of that has to do with belonging. If people do not have a sense that they belong in a larger culture they will cling in some way to increasingly imagined roots. In that kind of a setting the immigrant community and the home community can drift further and further apart. Nothing amazes me more than the Irish coming to Chicago on March 17 to participate in Saint Patrick's Day festivities. It is no big deal in Ireland, but you would never guess that from the way it is celebrated in this country, an example of how imaginings move us in different directions.

The third set of remappings, grew particularly out of the issues of conflict and suffering, developing into what might be called praxological models — that is to say, ways of negotiating religious pluralism that move beyond talk and more firmly into action. Ruiz again emphasized the vantage point of the poor,

Knitter spoke of the crucible of suffering, and Ronald Kidd spoke
of the importance of a path. Essentially what he was saying was
that while he appreciated Knitter's sense of moving religious pluralism from a focus on God to a focus on the earth, even that
didn't really resonate with his Buddhist sensibility, that it has to
be a much more open-ended sort of path.

The Future

Let me conclude with a look at the future. Five things which
emerged from this conference and call for action struck me as
constituting the agenda for the future. The first is that we need
all of us to reexplore the traditions out of which we come. This
point was made initially and perhaps most strongly by Raimon
Panikkar. We need to look at the apparent polarities, incom-
mensurabilities, cosmologies that shape our understanding of our
traditions, where we come from. As our boundaries shift and
our perceptions shift, so too do our points of entry into those
traditions. Both Arthur Waskow and Ali Jaffrey, speaking out
of the Jewish and Zoroastrian traditions, respectively, made this
same point. They saw themselves as creating a renewal movement
within those two traditions, as a way of grasping more firmly
the authentic roots out of which they came, the authentic roots
that nourished them in a changed world. Dr. Nasr's metaphor
of the tree here was particularly useful, that we are all branches
of a tree; we cannot survive without the trunk or the roots, a
particularity that continues to change as it interacts with other
realities.

A second piece of agenda that seems to me to emerge out of
the discussions here is perhaps a response to something Dr. Nasr
said this morning about dialogue being primarily a Western pre-
occupation. I would suggest we need to look at some of the
non-Western and nonmodern models of dialogue. One that came
to mind immediately when he said that is a Western one but certainly a nonmodern one; it comes out of Spain in the thirteenth
century. Raimon Llul wrote a book whose title would be translated (though the book has not been translated) as *The Book of
the Pagan and the Three Wise Men*. The three sages in this in-

stance were a Jew, a Muslim, and a Christian and all three of them were trying to convince this other individual, a Gentile, that their way of belief was the best. Llul himself was a Christian. But interestingly enough, at the end of the dialogue, the Christian doesn't win. There are other models perhaps we have to look at, attempts of faiths to explain themselves to each other. One that I found particularly fascinating is the second wave of the Nestorian movement into China, and the attempts there to understand in different sorts of ways. We have models from Muslim history. How was it that Peoples of the Book were able to get along under the caliphate in Baghdad, in a way that those three communities no longer are able to?

A third set of issues for us to look to in the future, I think, is that we need to study situations of conflict and violence perhaps by way of some case studies. I think we have had three remarkable ones in the course of this conference, one provided by Samuel Ruiz, who, in speaking of the evangelization of the native peoples in this hemisphere, talked about what these people underwent in this process. There are some case studies in there. Clara Sue Kidwell's discussion of the Choctaw in this country and Christian missionaries provides a marvelous example of two sets of people in an encounter with each other in which there is very little understanding of the other, the Choctaw trying certainly on their part, the white colonizers very little. I've already mentioned Gurinder Singh Mann's discussion of the encounter between Sikh, Hindu, and Muslim, which, over a period of nearly half a millennium, has become a story of conflict and violence. What can these tell us about communities coming into confrontation with each other?

The fourth piece of agenda, I suggest, is that we need to explore how identities can be built on pluralism rather than sameness. Certainly one issue that was raised in the second day of this conference has to be central here, that without justice no identity can be built on pluralism, that the differing parts in contact with each other must exist in an atmosphere of justice. So justice is the sine qua non. We need also to look at what constitutes certainty and security for people. Some of you may recall the questions that came at the very end of the discussion with

Raimon Panikkar. What about people who come to religious traditions looking for security and then we say that in the pluralistic contact you are not going to have that security? What do we do in this sort of a situation? We need to explore that more. What are the rules of hospitality, the rules of dialogue in all of this?

And finally, the fifth piece of agenda that I would suggest to us is that we need to continue to search for our common and uncommon ground. Is there a *religio perennis?* I am not as convinced of that as Frithjof Schuon, but that does not mean that we should stop looking. What does constitute the common ground we share? Is it a risk? Is it the threat of survival? In other words, is it best expressed ethically? What is our common ground? And at the same time we need to search together our uncommon ground, and I'm using that particularly in the sense of the uncommonly wonderful and beautiful things that all of our traditions try to touch, that area that Panikkar called mystery, that others call the transcendent. Without keeping in constant touch with that, without being fed and formed by that reality, our struggle to deal with, understand, negotiate, and enact a genuine pluralism is bound to wither and die. This has been an extraordinarily rich conference. Have we moved to new ground? I think we have, and I have tried to point out where some of that is. It's been a conference which, I think, was marked by people who are willing to disagree, by people who are willing to share their story, by people who are willing to try to think through the hard realities that we face and the changing world in which we live. Thank you.

Contributors

Masao Abe was born in Japan and now lives in Kyoto. A leading interpreter of Buddhism, he is also a prominent participant in Christian-Buddhist dialogue. His key essay "Kenotic God and Dynamic Śūnyatā" appears in John B. Cobb, Jr., ed., *The Emptying of God: A Buddhist-Jewish-Christian Conversation* (1990), and his book *Zen and Western Thought* (1985) won the American Academy of Religion Award for outstanding contribution to scholarship in religion.

Julia Ching is University Professor and the R. C. and E. Y. Lee Chair Professor at the University of Toronto. Her books include *Confucianism and Christianity: A Comparative Study* (1977); *Discovering China: European Interpretations in the Enlightenment* (1992), and, most recently, *Mysticism and Kingship in China* (1997).

Harvey Cox is Victor S. Thomas Professor of Divinity at Harvard University. His best-known work is *The Secular City* (1965). His other works include *The Feast of Fools* (1969); *The Seduction of the Spirit* (1973); *Turning East* 1977); and *Many Mansions: A Christian's Encounter with Other Faiths* (1988). He is an ordained Baptist minister.

Kathleen M. Dugan is a professor of Theological and Religious studies at the University of San Diego. In her career there she taught broadly in the field of religious studies, centering her research and teaching on contemporary Catholic theology and its dialogue with the world's religious traditions.

Clara Sue Kidwell is the Director of the Native American Studies program at the University of Oklahoma in Norman.

Paul F. Knitter is Professor of Theology at Xavier University. His books include *No Other Name?: A Critical Survey of Christian Attitudes towards Other Religions* (1985); *The Myth of Christian Uniqueness* (1987); and *Faith, Religion, and Theology: A Contemporary Introduction* (1990).

Donald W. Mitchell is Professor of Comparative Philosophy of Religion at Purdue University in Indiana. He is the author of *Spirituality and Emptiness: The Dynamics of Spiritual Life in Buddhism and Christianity* and editor of *Masao Abe: A Zen Life in Dialogue*.

Seyyed Hossein Nasr was born in Iran. From 1958 to 1979 he was Professor of Philosophy at Tehran University. He became the Professor of Islamic Studies at Temple University in 1979 and is presently University Professor of Islamic Studies at George Washington University. He delivered the Gifford lectures in 1981, which have been published under the title *Knowledge and the Sacred*. His other works include *Ideals and Realities of Islam* (1966) and *Traditional Islam in the Modern World* (1987).

Raimon Panikkar lives in Tavertet, Spain, after having taught for several years at the University of California, Santa Barbara. His books include *Unknown Christ of Hinduism* (1964); *The Vedic Experience: Mantramanjari: An Anthology of the Vedas for Modern and Contemporary Celebration* (1977); and *The Silence of God: The Answer of the Buddha* (1990).

Samuel Ruiz García is the bishop of San Cristóbal de las Casas, Chiapas, Mexico.

Robert J. Schreiter teaches in the Department of Theology at the Catholic Theological Union in Chicago. He is the author of *The New Catholicity: Theology between the Global and the Local* (1997).

Arvind Sharma was born in India and is Professor of Comparative Religion at McGill University, Montreal, Canada. He is the author of *The Hindu Gītā* (1986); *A Hindu Perspective on the Philosophy of Religion* (1990); the editor of a trilogy on women and religion: *Women in World Religions* (1987); *Religion and Women* (1993); and *Today's Woman in World Religions* (1993); and recently published *The Concept of Universal Religion in Modern Hindu Thought* (1998).

Index

Abe, Masao, 2, 30, 62, 65, 137, 148, 150, 151, 187
Abel, 72
absolute, 155, 163, 171, 173
acculturation, 71
Africa, 90
Agapê, 42
al-Aḥad, 171
Aham brahman, 38
Albright, W. F., 137
Allah, 138,
Allāhu akbar, 170
alter ego, 16
altruism, 112
America, 155, 163
American Indians, 155, 167
anātmavāda, 43, 139
ancestors, 11
anthropocentrism, 67
aporias, 33, 36
Aquinas, Thomas, 169
Arabic, 63
Asian Americans, 12
Asian Immigration Act of 1965, 182
ātmavāda, 43
Aufhebung, 31, 33
Augustine, 36, 176
Australia, 180
avatars, 174
al-Ayyūbī, Ṣalāḥ al-Dīn, 159

Babri Mosque, 165
Baghdad, 193
Baha'i, 39, 189
Balkans, 10, 27
Bangladesh, 163, 164
Being, 31
believers, 53
Berry, Thomas, 119, 120, 122, 126
Bible, 13, 41, 45, 68, 89, 95–97, 99
bodhisattvas, 40
Bolivia, 27
Bonaventure, 36
Bonhoeffer, Dietrich, 19, 20, 49
Bosnia, 165
Boulding, Elise, 113

Brahmā, 142
Brahman, 138
Buddha, 138, 144, 173
Buddhism, 65, 138, 153, 167
Buddhists, 184
Burrows, William, 134

Cady, Linnel, 136
Cain, 72
California, 167
Calvinists, 38, 78, 79
Canada, 189
Capra, Fritjof, 119
Carlson, Jeffrey, 2, 179
caste system, 54, 55
Catholics, 60, 64, 101, 153, 170, 188
Central Asia, 10
Chesterton, G. K., 88
Chiapas, 90
Chicago, 2, 28, 59, 191
Chicago Divinity School, 15
Chickasaws, 75, 83
China, 11, 14, 15, 63, 65, 177, 183, 193
Chinese Buddhism, 13
Ching, Julia, 2, 4, 7, 189, 191
Choctaws, 71–87, 193
Christ, 65, 95, 155, 173
Christ, Carol, 112
Christianity, 16, 27, 48, 61, 169, 172
Christian missions, 71ff., 77
Christians, 34, 37, 44, 91, 163, 168
Chuang Chou, 7, 16
Church, 25, 92, 97
Civilization Act of 1819, 76
civil religion, 57
clash of civilizations, 62
CNN, 152
Colombia, 27
compassion, 147
Confucianism, 16, 31, 65, 138
conversion, 11, 23, 51, 61, 83, 92, 97, 133
Cordoba, 153
Cox, Harvey, 3, 48, 56–59, 188
Crawford, S. Cromwell, 4

Creeks, 75, 83
crosscultural criteria, 128ff

Dalai Lama, 135
Dante Alighieri, 41
Dasein, 17
Davaney, Sheila Greeve, 121
Day of Judgment, 154
D'Costa, Gavin, 113
Decalogue, 89, 125
Derrett, J. Duncan M., 55
Dharma, 36, 113, 117, 138
dialectics, 32
dialogue, 49, 50, 51, 56, 60, 65, 94, 104ff, 131, 137, 188
DiNoia, Joseph, 113
Donovan, Peter, 135
dreams, 7–8, 18, 19
dualism, 30
duality, 15

earth, 114, 118
Earth Charter, 119, 125
East, 13
Eck, Diana, 182, 184, 190, 191
eclecticism, 25, 26
ecumenism, 58
ego, 112, 113
egocentrism, 67
Egypt, 89
Elder, John C., 125
elitism, 52
El Salvador, 117, 184
epochê, 32
Erikson, Erik H., 10, 14
ethics, 68, 114
ethnic, 54
Eucharist, 94, 172
Europe, 60, 155
evangelization, 93, 188
evolutionism, 24
exclusivism, 24

faith, 57
feminism, 64, 103, 112
Fiorenza, Francis Schüssler, 130
France, 59, 175
French Canadians, 12
Fuller, R. H., 9
fundamentalism, 55, 182, 188

Gandhi, Indira, 55
Gandhi, Mahatma, 44, 55, 108, 109

García, Samuel Ruiz, 3, 88, 185, 186, 189, 191, 193
Germany, 4, 183
global ethic, 187
globality, 55, 63, 104, 152, 157, 189
globalization, 4, 183
God, 9, 11, 13, 20, 34, 79, 52, 53, 57, 61, 67, 80, 81, 93, 95, 113, 138, 140, 144, 154, 160, 168, 177
Gospel, 94, 155
goy, 37
grace, 52
Greek Orthodoxy, 60
Guatemala, 183

ḥadīth, 158, 166
Halakah, 173
ḥanīf, 166
Harvard University, 58, 169, 173
Harvey, V., 108
Heaven, 176
Hegel, G. W. F., 32
Heidegger, Martin, 17
Heiler, F., 137
hermeneutics of suspicion, 112
Hick, John, 112
hierarchy, 102
Hinduism, 37–38, 45, 53, 138, 156, 157
history, 69–70
"history of religions," 1
hokma, 146
Holy Spirit, 99
Honen, 59
Horace, 179
human rights, 100

Ibo, 38
Ibsen, Henrik, 41
identities, multiple, 12
identity, 10, 156, 189, 191
identity crisis, 10
incommensurability, 129, 190
India, 27, 56, 118, 155, 156, 159, 165, 182
Indians, 89
Indian policy, 71
Indian Removal Act of 1830, 84
indifferentism, 25
indigenous religions, 92
insiders, 53
interfaith dialogue, 49
Iran, 156, 189
Ireland, 191

Ishtaboli, 75
Ishtahullo chito, 73
Islam, 30, 38, 57, 64, 153, 154
Italians, 183

Jaffrey, Ali, 182, 192
James, St., 41
Japan, 50, 65, 187
Japanese Buddhism, 168
Jefferson, Thomas, 72
Jewishness, 38, 145, 193
Jews, 9, 28, 153, 155, 163
Joan of Arc, 11, 20
John XXIII, Pope, 96
John of the Cross, 41, 175
Judaic law, 93
Judaism, 31, 102, 157, 170
Jung, Carl, 10, 14
justice, 42, 69, 106, 145, 193

Kabbalists, 159
kairos, 44
karma, 45, 132
karuṇā, 42, 117
Katz, Steven T., 112
Kaufman, Gordon D., 107
Keller, Catherine, 112
kenosis, 68, 150
Kidd, Ronald, 186, 192
Kidwell, Clara Sue, 3, 71, 193
King, Sallie, 112, 113
Kitagawa, Joseph, 15
Knitter, Paul F., 3, 4, 104, 185, 186, 189, 190
Kuan-yin, 13
Kubose, Rev. Sunnan, 184
Küng, Hans, 104, 109, 140
Kyoto School, 149

Lang, A., 137
las Casas, Bartolomé de, 90
Latin America, 91
Law of Moses, 174
Lebensraum, 152
Leibholz, Gerhard, 20
Leishman, J. B., 20
liberals, 188
Lindbeck, George, 134
Lings, Martin, 154
Linton, Ralph, 71
Liu Xiaogan, 2, 53
Llul, Raimon, 192
Logos, 140, 166

Lonergan, Bernard, 133
Lutherans, 177

MacIntyre, Alasdair, 106
Macquarrie, John, 17
Mahdī, 154, 158
Mahmoudi, Hoda, 189
Maimonides, 159
Malay, 63
Mann, Gurinder Singh, 185, 189, 193
Manu, 173
Marcel, Gabriel, 8, 187
Marx, Karl, 9
Marxism, 31
Mary, 13, 103
Massignon, Louis, 58, 160
matrimony, 102
McDaniel, Jay, 119
McFague, Sallie, 119–21
Mencius, 19
Mendeleyev, Dmitry, 26
metanoia, 23, 47
Mexico, 183–84
Middle Ages, 153, 165
Middle East, 10
minority religion, 28
missionaries, 13, 157
Mississippi, 71, 73, 76, 81, 82, 84, 87
Mitchell, Donald W., 3, 137, 147, 150
modernity, 181
monotheism, 142
monotheistic religions, 144
Morocco, 58
Mounier, Emmanuel, 9
Mulan, 11
Murdoch, Rupert, 183
Mushulatubbee, 82
Muslims, 37, 51, 163
muṭlaq, 171
mysticism, 109

NAFTA, 99
Nasr, Seyyed Hossein, 3, 5, 57, 125, 152, 180, 181, 185, 186, 187, 190, 192
Native Americans, 125
Nazism, 41, 49
Nestorians, 193
Neusner, Jacob, 2
New York, 64, 163, 164, 170
Nicaragua, 101
Nichts, 137, 140, 149
nirvāṇa, 113, 139

nominalism, 164
Northern Ireland, 10, 37, 64

O'Hare, Madalyn Murray, 49
option for the poor, 99ff
ordination of women, 103
Ortega y Gasset, José, 41
Orthodox Judaism, 60
"Other," 34, 105

Pakistan, 63
Panikkar, Raimon, 2, 4, 23, 108, 160,
    181, 183, 185–87, 189, 191, 192,
    194
parable, 24
Parliament of Religions, 24, 33, 50,
    104, 105, 155
Parliament of World's Religions, 2, 48,
    88, 104, 155, 179, 187
Parmenides, 32
Parsi, 28
partition of India, 163
Pascal, Blaise, 42
Patañjali, 177
Paul VI, Pope, 96
Penelope, 2
Pentecostal Christianity, 188
perichoresis, 150
Persia, 63
personal identity, 7, 10, 36
Peter the Venerable, 174
philosophia perennis, 166
phronesis, 134
Pieris, Aloysius, 107
Pithecanthropus erectus, 25
Pittsburgh, 182
pizza, 183
Plaskow, Judith, 112
pluralism, 1, 25–26, 28ff, 30, 56, 180
plurality, 1, 30
polygamy, 78
postmodern criticism, 105, 123, 129,
    130, 135, 155, 190
pratītya-samutpāda, 138
Presbyterians, 79, 80
primal religions, 157
progress, 98ff, 176
prophetic power, 109
prophets, 14
proselytization, 51
Protestant ethic, 72
Protestantism, 60
pseudo-values, 100
pūrvapakshin, 29

qiblah, 170
Quran, 41, 154, 166, 174, 178

rationalism, 32
rationality, 32
Redfield, Robert, 71
reductio ad unum, 36
relativism, 170
religion, 107, 109
religion, Abrahamic, 109
religion, academic study of, 160, 164
religion, Indic, 109
religion and culture, 29
religion and tradition, 29
Religionswissenschaft, 1
religio perennis, 58, 161, 166–71, 173,
    194
religious conflict, 88, 142
religious identity, 27, 35
religious peace, 35
religious pluralism, 1, 152
Renouvier, Charles-Bernard, 59
resurrection, 12, 18
Robinson, Edward, 17
Rockefeller, Steven C., 125
Ruether, Rosemary Radford, 119
Ruiz García, Samuel 3, 88, 185, 186,
    189, 191, 193
Rumi, 59
Russell, Bertrand, 164

sacred, 169, 175
Saint Patrick's Day, 191
salvation history, 89
Samartha, Stanley, 109
samsāra, 18, 139
sanātana dharma, 45
Sandinista movement, 101
Sangha, 184
Śaṅkarācārya, 59
Sanskrit, 66
Saudi Arabia, 166
Schillebeeckx, Edward, 115, 116
Schreiter, Robert J., 2, 30, 53, 62, 65,
    191
Schuon, Frithjof, 58, 161, 166, 171,
    186, 194
science, 120
scientism, 31
secularism, 56, 57, 108n8, 153
self, 7–8, 175
Serbo-Croat Muslims, 12
Shakespeare, William, 41
Sharī'ah, 171, 173

Sharma, Arvind, 2, 30, 53, 62, 65, 191
shilombish, 75
shilup, 75
Shinto, 54, 138
Sicily, 159, 165
Sikhs, 185, 190
Silicon Valley, 167
Sitz im Leben, 3
Śiva, 45, 142
Smart, Ninian, 108
Smith, W. C., 160
Sobrino, Jon, 117, 118
Solomon, 61
sophia, 146
sophia perennis, 160, 166, 169
soteria, 107, 114, 127
Spain, 89, 91, 159, 184
Spirit, 24, 107
Spretnak, Charlene, 119, 121, 124, 126
Sri Lankan Buddhism, 168
stereotypes, 55
story, 119ff, 123ff
Sudanese Christians, 12
Sufis, 63, 159, 174
Sun Dance, 172
śūnyatā, 66, 139, 147, 167
Swimme, Brian, 119, 120, 122

Tabriz, 152
Tangiers, 152
Tao, 113, 117
Taoism, 21, 30, 64, 138, 153, 167, 177
tathatā, 139
al-Tawḥīdu wāḥid, 173
Thailand, 27
theocentrism, 67
Third World, 96
Thomism, 170
thou, 34
Tile, C. P., 137
Tillich, Paul, 17, 20–22, 113
tolerance, 25, 190
Tolstoy, Leo, 50
Tracy, David, 108, 110, 127, 128, 133
traditions, 46, 54, 170
trika, 45

Trimūrti, 141
Trinity, 15, 64, 150, 172
Turkish, 63
Tu Wei-ming, 2, 62
Tzu, Chuang, 7, 16, 18, 20, 22
Tzu, Lao, 41

umma, 25
United Kingdom, 57
United States, 27, 56, 180, 183, 187
unity, 142, 161–62
universality, 152
universal revelation, 122
universals, 30, 54, 93, 105, 114, 122, 124, 126, 130, 156, 190
Upanishads, 153
Urdu, 63
Utah, 189

varṇa, 55
Vatican Council II, 13, 93, 95
Vedanta, 37, 153
Vishṇu, 142
Vivekananda, 157, 176

Wall Street, 64
Waskow, Arthur, 181, 189, 192
WASPs, 12
Watson, Burton, 8, 18, 20, 22
Weil, Simone, 44
West, 13, 63, 153, 158, 165, 167, 179, 180
West Coast, 182
Western Christianity, 25, 106
Western concerns, 106, 187, 192
Western religions, 137
Wilson, Edward O., 123
wisdom, 145, 146
Woods, Ralph, 16
World Parliament of Religions, 1, 2, 23, 48, 50

Yahweh, 9, 89, 96, 138
Yoga Sūtra, 42, 177

Zen, 21
Zoroastrianism, 156, 182